What's Cooking

stir-fry

What's Cooking

stir-fry

A collection of must-have recipes for all occasions

First published in 2010

LOVE FOOD is an imprint of Parragon Books Ltd

Parragon
Queen Street House
4 Queen Street
Bath BA1 1HE, UK

ISBN: 978-1-4454-0319-9

Printed in China

Cover design by Talking Design
Cover image by Clive Streeter
Internal design by Simon Levy
Additional photography by Charlie Richards
Additional home economy by Anna Burges-Lumsden, assisted by Mima Sinclair
Introduction and additional recipes by Christine McFadden

Notes for the Reader

This book uses both metric and imperial measurements. Follow the same units of measurement throughout; do not mix metric and imperial. All spoon measurements are level: teaspoons are assumed to be 5 ml, and tablespoons are assumed to be 15 ml. Unless otherwise stated, milk is assumed to be full fat, eggs and individual vegetables are medium, and pepper is freshly ground black pepper.

The times given are an approximate guide only. Preparation times differ according to the techniques used by different people and the cooking times may also vary from those given. Optional ingredients, variations or serving suggestions have not been included in the calculations.

Recipes using raw or very lightly cooked eggs should be avoided by infants, the elderly, pregnant women, convalescents and anyone suffering from an illness. Pregnant and breastfeeding women are advised to avoid eating peanuts and peanut products. Sufferers from nut allergies should be aware that some of the ready-made ingredients used in the recipes in this book may contain nuts. Always check the packaging before use.

Vegetarians should be aware that some of the ready-made ingredients used in the recipes in this book may contain animal products. Always check the packaging before use.

CONTENTS

INTRODUCTION

The workhorse of the Chinese kitchen, the wok has been in use for over 2000 years. The basic shape remains unchanged, and it is still the essential cooking vessel in the poorest of homes and the most luxurious of restaurants.

Historically, cooking vessels evolved for a number of reasons, a key issue being the type of fuel available. This, in turn, dictated the design and the type of food that could be cooked. In China, fuel was mainly wood, charcoal or animal dung. Supplies were meagre and unpredictable, and much of Chinese cuisine is therefore based on poverty and coping with the harsh conditions commonplace in a predominately agrarian society. The cooking method had to make efficient use of whatever precious fuel was available, and the pan had to heat up quickly. The wok's conical shape and high flaring sides were a masterpiece of design in that respect. Made of metal, it conducted heat quickly, creating a small but intensely hot area at the base. This made it possible for bite-sized morsels of food to be quickly stir-fried using relatively little fuel and cooking oil.

The wok was designed for use over the traditional Chinese pit stove – a charcoal or wood fire set below a rectangular 'fire bench' in which round holes or pits were recessed to hold the wok in place. The wok sat snugly in the holes, the wide flaring sides preventing it from dropping into the fire below. The heat rising from the fuel was fully directed to the bottom of the wok, and no heat escaped round the edges.

Nowadays, pit-style stoves are heated with natural gas, but they follow the same principle with concentrically sloping grates or burners recessed below the stove's surface. The stoves in restaurants and communal kitchens can accommodate gigantic woks for boiling water and cooking huge quantities of rice or soup. At the other end of the scale, the wok may be used over the simplest of braziers, which were, and still are, the mainstay of the kitchen for poverty-stricken families.

MULTI-PURPOSE COOKING VESSEL

Thanks to its unique shape, the wok can cope with virtually all types of food and cooking techniques. Once the base is hot, the heat spreads through the entire inside surface, creating a far greater cooking surface than Western pots and pans with vertical sides. This in turn creates a range of cooking temperatures in one pan – pieces of food that have been seared in the bottom of the wok can be pushed up the sides to continue cooking at a slower rate. Meanwhile, another ingredient for the same dish is added and cooked at high heat in the bottom.

Though most often used for stir-frying, the wok can also be used for steaming, boiling, braising, deep-frying, shallow-frying and smoking.

There are two basic wok designs, the Cantonese and the Pau or Peking, both of which are used throughout China. The Cantonese has two rounded handles that make it easier to use when full of liquid – during steaming or deep-frying, for example. The Pau wok has one long handle and is more convenient, and safer too, for stir-frying. The pan is held in one hand and shaken while the food is turned with a long-handled ladle or spoon held in the other. The long handle distances the cook from the intense heat and hot oil. Some long-handled woks have a small round handle on the opposite side, which comes in handy when carrying the hot wok from stove to table.

MATERIALS

Woks were traditionally made of cast-iron, which maintains a steady even heat. It is worth noting that Chinese cast-iron woks are thinner and lighter than the Western equivalent. They heat up more quickly and also form a more stable layer of seasoning that prevents food from sticking. The downside is that they are prone to shattering if mishandled or dropped. Western cast-iron woks, on the other hand, are sturdier but slow to heat up and cool down, making all-important temperature control during stir-frying more difficult.

Currently, the most widely used material is carbon steel. Steel woks are relatively light in weight, conduct heat evenly and are quick to heat up. However, they vary widely in price and quality. The best are made with two sheets of carbon steel that are formed into shape by hand hammering. You can spot them by the small ridges and dimples on the inside of the wok. The lowest quality are stamped from a single sheet of steel and likely to distort after a while.

HEALTH BENEFITS

Thanks to its versatility, the wok can be used for healthy ways of cooking. Stir-frying allows you to enjoy the pleasure of fried food without an unhealthy amount of oil. Unlike a standard frying pan with a wide flat base, the wok requires very little oil to lubricate the food – all that's needed is a tablespoon or so in the base. If you're counting calories, you can even use non-stick cooking spray. Because of the high temperature the food cooks very quickly without soaking up oil. Once cooked, it is pushed up the sloping sides of the wok and the oil drains back to the bottom.

Steaming is another healthy option and is easy to do in a wok. It is perfect for vegetables and tender items such as fish and chicken. The moist environment means no fat is needed, and fewer nutrients leach into the cooking water since the food does not come in contact with it.

Stewing and braising are also possible in a wok. From a health point of view, fewer nutrients are lost, and fat can be kept to a minimum.

BASIC RECIPES

BASIC CHINESE STOCK

Makes about 1.5 litres/2³/₄ pints

Ingredients
900 kg/2 lb chicken pieces, such as wings,
    thighs and drumsticks, roughly chopped
900 kg/2 lb pork spare ribs
450 kg/1 lb ham or unsmoked gammon without
rind, in one piece
4 litres/7 pints water
7 cm/2³/₄ inch thick piece fresh ginger,
unpeeled and thickly sliced
1 celery stalk, roughly chopped
1 carrot, roughly chopped
3 large spring onions, green parts included,
    halved lengthways
2 tsp Chinese rice wine or dry sherry

1 Put the chicken, pork and ham in a large
  saucepan and just cover with water. Quickly
  bring to the boil, then drain in a colander and
  rinse away the scum under cold running water.
  Wash out the pan.

2 Return the meat to the pan and cover with the
  4 litres/7 pints of water. Add the ginger,
  celery, carrot and spring onions, and slowly
  bring back to the boil, skimming off any
  further scum that forms. Reduce the heat
  to a very gentle simmer and cook, uncovered,
  for 2 hours.

3 Strain the stock through a colander, reserving
  the liquid and discarding the solids. Pour
  the liquid through a muslin-lined sieve.
  Pour back into the pan and add the rice
  wine. Bring to the boil, then simmer for
  2–3 minutes.

4 Pour into containers, leave to cool, then store
  in the refrigerator. Once thoroughly chilled,
  remove the solidified fat from the surface.

SPICY BEEF STOCK

Makes about 1.5 litres/2³/₄ pints

Ingredients
1.5 kg/3 lb 5 oz beef brisket or boneless shin of
beef, cut into large chunks
3 litres/5¹/₄ pints water
1 small onion, quartered
5 cm/2 inch thick piece fresh ginger, unpeeled
    and thickly sliced
5 cm/2 inch cinnamon stick
5 star anise pods
1 tsp black peppercorns
1 tsp salt

1 Put the beef in a large saucepan with enough
  water to cover. Quickly bring to the boil, then
  drain in a colander and rinse away the scum
  under cold running water. Wash out the pan.

2 Return the meat to the saucepan with the
  3 litres/5¹/₄ pints of water, the onion,
  ginger, cinnamon stick, star anise, black
  peppercorns and salt. Slowly bring back to
  the boil, skimming off any further scum that
  forms. Reduce the heat to a very gentle
  simmer and cook, uncovered, for 2 hours.

3 Strain the stock through a colander, reserving
  the liquid and discarding the solids. Pour
  the liquid through a muslin-lined sieve. Pour
  into containers, leave to cool, then store in the
  refrigerator. Once thoroughly chilled, remove
  the solidified fat from the surface.

SPRING ONION DIPPING SAUCE

Ingredients
4 tbsp finely chopped spring onions
4 tbsp finely chopped fresh ginger
2 tbsp light soy sauce
1 tsp rice vinegar
4 tbsp rapeseed oil

1 Combine the ingredients in a bowl and whisk very thoroughly until well blended. For a smooth sauce, purée in a blender.

SOY-GINGER DIPPING SAUCE

Ingredients
3 tbsp soy sauce
2 tsp very finely chopped fresh ginger

1 Combine the soy sauce and ginger in a small serving bowl. Leave to stand for 15 minutes to let the flavour develop.

SPICED SALT AND PEPPER

Ingredients
1 tbsp Szechuan pepper
1 tsp white peppercorns
5 cm/2 inch cinnamon stick, broken
2 star anise pods
5 tbsp sea salt flakes
1 tsp sugar

1 Dry-fry the Szechuan pepper, white peppercorns, cinnamon and star anise in a wok over medium heat, shaking the pan, until the Szechuan pepper begins to smoke and smell fragrant. Grind to a coarse powder with the salt, using an electric coffee grinder or a hefty mortar and pestle. Stir in the sugar then store in an airtight container for up to 2 months.

TO START

VIETNAMESE BEEF & NOODLE SOUP

Purée the shallots, garlic and ginger in a food processor or blender, pulsing several times until the purée is fairly smooth.

Heat a wok over a medium–high heat, then add the oil and stir-fry the paste for 2 minutes, taking care not to let it burn. Add the beef and stir-fry for 1 minute until brown, then pour in 1 litre/1¾ pints of the stock. Bring to a rolling boil, skimming off any scum that forms. Add the crushed peppercorns, then reduce the heat and gently simmer for 30–35 minutes, or until the meat is tender.

Meanwhile, soak the noodles in enough lukewarm water to cover for 15 minutes, or cook according to the instructions on the packet, until soft.

When the meat is tender, stir in any sticky residue that has formed at the edge of the wok. Add the remaining stock, the lime juice, fish sauce, salt and sugar. Simmer for a few minutes.

Drain the noodles and divide between individual soup bowls. Ladle the meat and broth over the top. Serve with the garnishes sprinkled over the soup.

SERVES 4

4 shallots, chopped

1 large garlic clove, chopped

2 tsp finely chopped fresh ginger

1 tbsp groundnut oil

450 g/1 lb sirloin steak, external fat removed, cut into 1-cm/½-inch cubes

1.3 litres/2¼ pints Spicy Beef Stock (see page 8)

1 tsp white peppercorns, crushed

150 g/5½ oz flat rice noodles

juice of 1 lime

2 tsp Thai fish sauce

½ tsp salt

½ tsp sugar

to garnish

4 spring onions, shredded

slivers of red chilli

3 tbsp torn coriander leaves

3 tbsp torn basil leaves

lime wedges

SPICY BEEF & MUSHROOM WONTONS

To make the filling, combine the minced steak, spring onion, mushrooms, garlic and ginger in a bowl. Mix the soy sauce, salt, pepper, five-spice seasoning and cornflour to a thin paste. Add the paste to the beef mixture, then stir in half the beaten egg (use the remainder in another recipe). Stir with a fork until very well mixed.

Separate the wonton squares and place on a tray, rotating them so one corner is facing towards you. Cover with a clean damp tea towel to prevent cracking. Working with one square at a time, place a slightly rounded teaspoon of filling in the bottom corner 1 cm/½ inch away from the point. Fold the point over the filling, then roll up two thirds of the wrapper, leaving a point at the top. Moisten the right- and left-hand corners with a dab of water. Fold one corner over the other and press lightly to seal into a bishop's mitre shape. Continue until all the wontons are filled.

Heat a large wok over a high heat. Pour in the oil and heat to 180°C/350°F or until a cube of bread browns in 30 seconds. Deep-fry the wontons in batches for 4–5 minutes until golden brown. Remove with tongs and drain on crumpled kitchen paper. Serve with the dipping sauce.

MAKES 12–15

12–15 square wonton wrappers

groundnut oil, for deep-frying

Soy-Ginger Dipping Sauce (see page 9), to serve

filling

125 g/4 oz lean sirloin or rump steak, minced

1 spring onion, green part included, finely chopped

2 button mushrooms, finely chopped

1 small garlic clove, finely chopped

½ tsp finely chopped fresh ginger

½ tsp soy sauce

¼ tsp salt

¼ tsp freshly ground white pepper

⅛ tsp Chinese five-spice seasoning

½ tsp cornflour

1 egg, beaten

HOT & SOUR PORK SOUP WITH BAMBOO SHOOTS

Remove the hard stalks from the mushrooms and slice the caps very thinly. Cut the slices in half.

Bring the stock to a rolling boil in a large wok. Reduce the heat, add the mushrooms and simmer for 5 minutes. Add the pork, bamboo shoots and tofu, and simmer for a further 5 minutes. Add the rice wine, soy sauce, vinegar and white pepper, and simmer for 1 minute.

Ladle into soup bowls and sprinkle with the spring onions and a few drops of sesame oil.

SERVES 4

2 large shiitake mushrooms

1.25 litres/2¼ pints Basic Chinese Stock (see page 8)

125 g/4½ oz pork tenderloin, thinly sliced into narrow shreds

25 g/1 oz canned sliced bamboo shoots, drained

100 g/3½ oz firm tofu, cut into 1-cm/½-inch cubes

1 tbsp Chinese rice wine or dry sherry

2 tsp light soy sauce

1 tbsp rice vinegar

¼ tsp freshly ground white pepper, or more to taste

2 spring onions, some green included, thinly sliced diagonally, to garnish

few drops sesame oil, to garnish

PORK & PRAWN SPRING ROLLS

Squeeze out any excess water from the mushrooms and finely slice, discarding any tough stems.

Heat a wok over a medium–high heat, then add the oil. Stir-fry the pork until it changes colour. Add the soy sauce, bamboo shoots, mushrooms and salt. Stir over a high heat for 3 minutes.

Add the prawns and cook for 2 minutes, then add the beansprouts and cook for a further minute. Remove from the heat, stir in the spring onions and set aside to cool.

Place a tablespoon of the mixture towards the bottom of a spring roll wrapper. Roll once to secure the filling, then fold in the sides to create a 10-cm/4-inch width and continue to roll up. Seal with egg white.

Heat a large wok over a high heat. Pour in the oil and heat to 180°C/350°F or until a cube of bread browns in 30 seconds. Without overcrowding the pan, fry the rolls for about 5 minutes, until golden brown and crispy. Drain well on kitchen paper and and serve immediately with chilli sauce.

MAKES 20–25

6 dried Chinese mushrooms, soaked in warm water for 20 minutes

1 tbsp vegetable or groundnut oil, plus extra for deep-frying

225 g/8 oz pork mince

1 tsp dark soy sauce

100 g/3½ oz canned bamboo shoots, rinsed and julienned

pinch of salt

100 g/3½ oz prawns, peeled, deveined and chopped

225 g/8 oz fresh beansprouts, roughly chopped

1 tbsp finely chopped spring onions

25 spring roll wrappers

1 egg white, lightly beaten

chilli sauce, to serve

FRIED LAMB BALLS WITH SPRING ONION SAUCE

Combine the lamb, garlic and ginger in a bowl. Mix the soy sauce, wine, salt, sugar, pepper, and cornflour to a thin paste. Add the paste to the lamb mixture, then stir in the beaten egg. Stir with a fork until very well mixed. Pinch off small pieces of mixture and roll between your palms to form balls the size of a large marble.

Heat a wok over a high heat, add the oil and when it is almost smoking add the balls. Fry the balls in batches for 3 minutes, turning half-way through. Drain on crumpled kitchen paper.

Arrange a bed of shredded Chinese leaves on a serving platter. Arrange the lamb balls on top, and sprinkle with garlic chives. Divide the dipping sauce between two small bowls and serve with the lamb.

MAKES 36

450 g minced lamb

1 garlic clove, finely chopped

1 tsp finely chopped fresh ginger

1½ tbsp soy sauce

1 tsp Chinese rice wine or
   dry sherry

½ tsp salt

½ tsp sugar

½ tsp freshly ground white pepper

½ tbsp cornflour

1 egg, beaten

groundnut oil, for frying

snipped garlic chives, to garnish

shredded Chinese leaves, to serve

Spring Onion Dipping Sauce
   (see page 9), to serve

CHICKEN NOODLE SOUP

Cook the noodles in a saucepan of boiling water for 4 minutes, or according to the instructions on the packet, until soft.

Heat a wok over a medium–high heat, then add the oil. Add the chicken and stir-fry for 5 minutes, or until lightly browned. Add the white part of the spring onions, the garlic and ginger and stir-fry for 2 minutes.

Add the stock, coconut milk, curry paste, peanut butter and soy sauce. Season to taste with salt and pepper. Bring to the boil, stirring constantly, then simmer for 8 minutes, stirring occasionally. Add the pepper, peas and green spring onion tops and cook for a further 2 minutes.

Drain the noodles, then add them to the wok and heat through. Spoon into soup bowls and serve immediately.

SERVES 4–6

250 g/9 oz medium egg noodles

1 tbsp corn oil

4 skinless, boneless chicken thighs, diced

1 bunch of spring onions, sliced, white and green kept separate

2 garlic cloves, chopped

2-cm/³⁄₄-inch piece fresh ginger, finely chopped

850 ml/1¹⁄₂ pints chicken stock

175 ml/6 fl oz coconut milk

3 tsp Thai red curry paste

3 tbsp peanut butter

2 tbsp light soy sauce

1 small red pepper, deseeded and chopped

55 g/2 oz frozen peas

salt and pepper

ORIENTAL GLAZED CHICKEN WINGS

To make the marinade, combine the wine, soy sauce and vinegar in a small bowl. Add the sugar, salt and five-spice seasoning, and stir until dissolved. Mix in the hoisin sauce and ginger.

Put the chopped chicken wings in a shallow dish and pour in the marinade, turning the wings to coat. Leave to marinate for 1 hour at room temperature, or overnight in the refrigerator.

Heat a wok over a high heat, add the oil and when it is almost smoking add the chicken wings and marinade. Stir-fry for 5 minutes, then sprinkle with 4 tablespoons of the stock and stir-fry for a further 4 minutes.

Using tongs, transfer the wings to a warmed serving dish, and sprinkle with the coriander. Pour off and discard most of the oil from the wok and return to the heat. Add the remaining 2 tablespoons of stock, and stir with a wooden spoon until blended, scraping up the sticky sediment. Pour into a small bowl and serve with the wings as a dipping sauce.

SERVES 4

8 chicken wings, each wing chopped into 3 pieces

5 tbsp groundnut oil

6 tbsp Basic Chinese Stock (see page 8) or water

2 tbsp chopped fresh coriander

marinade

1½ tbsp Chinese rice wine or dry sherry

1 tbsp soy sauce

1 tbsp rice vinegar

1½ tbsp sugar

¾ tsp salt

⅛ tsp Chinese five-spice seasoning

3 tbsp hoisin sauce

1 tsp finely chopped fresh ginger

SHREDDED DUCK WITH CUCUMBER

Stack the cucumber slices, cut into thin strips and set aside. Combine the sauce ingredients in a small bowl, stirring to dissolve the sugar.

Heat a wok over a medium–high heat, then add the oils. Fry the duck breast pieces for 4–5 minutes, starting skin-side down and turning occasionally until both the skin and meat are crisp. Transfer with tongs to a cutting board and leave to cool slightly.

Lower the heat to medium. Stir-fry the shallot and ginger in the remaining oil for about 2 minutes until golden brown. Remove with a slotted spoon and drain on kitchen paper.

Remove the crisp skin from the duck pieces, and slice into shreds. Remove and discard any excess fat from the meat. Slice the meat into 5-mm/¼-inch-wide strips.

Wipe out the wok with kitchen paper and place over a medium–high heat. Add the duck meat, sauce and spring onions, and stir-fry for 2 minutes until caramelised. Season with salt and pepper, then remove from the heat.

Divide the duck mixture between the lettuce leaves, top with the cucumber strips, shallot, ginger and crushed peanuts. Roll up into parcels and serve.

SERVES 4

5-cm/2-inch piece cucumber, peeled and thinly sliced

1 tbsp groundnut oil

1 tbsp sesame oil

2 duck breasts, weighing 350 g/12 oz in total, cut into large pieces

1 large shallot, halved and sliced into crescents

2 cm/¾ inch piece fresh ginger, thinly sliced and cut into shreds

2 spring onions, shredded

4 large Webbs lettuce leaves, stalks removed

25 g/1 oz dry roasted peanuts, crushed

salt and pepper

sauce

2 tsp soy sauce

4 tsp oyster sauce

2 tsp Chinese rice wine or dry sherry

¾ tsp sugar

THAI-STYLE SEAFOOD SOUP

Place the stock in a wok with the lemon grass, lime rind, ginger and chilli paste. Bring just to the boil, then reduce the heat and simmer, covered, for 10–15 minutes.

Cut the spring onions in half lengthways, then slice crossways very thinly. Cut the prawns almost in half lengthways, keeping the tails intact. Devein if necessary.

Pour the stock through a sieve, then return to the wok and bring to a simmer, with bubbles rising at the edges and the surface trembling. Add the spring onions and cook for 2–3 minutes. Taste and season with salt, if needed. Stir in a little more chilli paste, if wished.

Add the scallops and prawns and poach for 1 minute, or until they turn opaque and the prawns curl.

Drop in the coriander leaves, then ladle the soup into bowls, dividing the shellfish evenly, and garnish with chilli rings.

SERVES 4

1.25 litres/2¼ pints fish stock

1 lemon grass stem, split lengthways

pared rind of ½ lime or 1 fresh kaffir lime leaf

2.5-cm/1-inch piece fresh ginger, sliced

¼ tsp chilli paste, or to taste

4–6 spring onions

200 g/7 oz large or medium raw prawns, peeled

salt

250 g/9 oz scallops (16–20)

2 tbsp coriander leaves

fresh red chilli rings, to garnish

PRAWN TOASTS

Pound the prawns to a pulp in a mortar and pestle or with the base of a cleaver.

Mix the prawns with one of the egg whites and 1 tablespoon of the cornflour. Add the sugar and salt and stir in the coriander. Mix the remaining egg white with the remaining cornflour.

Remove the crusts from the bread and cut each slice into 8 triangles. Brush the top of each piece with the egg white and cornflour mixture, then add 1 teaspoon of the prawn mixture. Smooth the top.

Heat a large wok over a high heat. Pour in the oil and heat to 180°C/350°F or until a cube of bread browns in 30 seconds. Without overcrowding the wok, cook the toasts prawn-side up for about 2 minutes. Turn and cook for a further 2 minutes, or until beginning to turn golden brown. Drain and serve warm.

TO START

30

MAKES 16

100 g/3½ oz raw prawns, peeled and deveined

2 egg whites, kept separate

2 tbsp cornflour

½ tsp sugar

pinch of salt

2 tbsp finely chopped coriander leaves

2 slices day-old white bread

vegetable or groundnut oil, for deep-frying

CRISPY CRAB WONTONS

To make the filling, mix together the crabmeat, water chestnuts, chilli, spring onion, cornflour, sherry, soy sauce and lime juice in a bowl.

Spread out the wonton wrappers on a work surface and spoon an equal portion of the filling into the centre of each wonton wrapper.

Dampen the edges of the wonton wrappers with a little water and fold them in half to form triangles. Fold the 2 pointed ends in towards the centre, moisten with a little water to secure, then pinch together to seal.

Heat a large wok over a high heat. Pour in the oil and heat to 180ºC/350ºF or until a cube of bread browns in 30 seconds. Deep-fry the wontons in batches for 2–3 minutes, until golden brown and crisp (if you deep-fry too many at one time, the oil temperature will drop and they will be soggy).

Remove the wontons with a slotted spoon, drain on kitchen paper and serve hot, garnished with chives and lime slices.

MAKES 24

175 g/6 oz white crabmeat, drained if canned and thawed if frozen, flaked

50 g/1¾ oz canned water chestnuts, drained, rinsed, and chopped

1 small fresh red chilli, chopped

1 spring onion, chopped

1 tbsp cornflour

1 tsp dry sherry

1 tsp light soy sauce

½ tsp lime juice

24 wonton wrappers

vegetable oil, for deep-frying

fresh chives, to garnish

lime slices, to garnish

MUSHROOM & GINGER SOUP

Soak the dried Chinese mushrooms for at least 30 minutes in 300 ml/10 fl oz of the hot stock. Drain the mushrooms and reserve the stock. Remove the stalks of the mushrooms and discard. Slice the caps and reserve.

Cook the noodles in a saucepan of boiling water for 4 minutes, or according to the instructions on the packet, until soft. Drain well, rinse under cold water, and drain again. Set aside.

Heat a wok over a high heat, then add the oil. Add the garlic and ginger, stir and add the mushrooms. Stir over a high heat for 2 minutes.

Add the remaining stock with the reserved stock and bring to the boil. Add the mushroom ketchup and soy sauce. Stir in the beansprouts and cook until tender.

Place some noodles in each soup bowl and ladle the soup on top. Garnish with fresh coriander sprigs and serve immediately.

SERVES 4

15 g/½ oz dried Chinese mushrooms

1 litre/1¾ pints hot vegetable stock

125 g/4½ oz fine egg noodles

2 tsp sunflower oil

3 garlic cloves, crushed

2.5-cm/1-inch piece fresh ginger, finely shredded

½ tsp mushroom ketchup

1 tsp light soy sauce

125 g/4½ oz fresh beansprouts

fresh coriander sprigs, to garnish

CRISPY 'SEAWEED'

Remove and discard the tough stalks from the cabbage leaves. Wash the leaves, drain thoroughly and spread out on kitchen paper to dry.

Stack a few leaves and roll up tightly. Using a very sharp knife, slice crossways into the thinnest possible shreds. Repeat with the remaining leaves. Spread out the shreds on kitchen paper and leave until completely dry.

Heat a large wok over a high heat. Pour in the oil and heat to 180°C/350°F or until a cube of bread browns in 30 seconds. Remove the wok from the heat and add half the shredded leaves. Return the wok to the heat and deep-fry until the shreds begin to float to the surface and become crisp. Remove with a slotted spoon and drain on kitchen paper. Keep warm while you deep-fry the rest.

Tip the shreds into a warm serving bowl. Combine the sugar and salt, and sprinkle over the 'seaweed', tossing to mix.

Quickly fry the flaked almonds in the hot oil. Remove with a slotted spoon and sprinkle over the 'seaweed'. Serve warm or at room temperature.

SERVES 4

250 g/9 oz dark green cabbage leaves

groundnut oil, for deep-frying

1 tsp caster sugar

½ tsp salt

4 tbsp flaked almonds, to garnish

VEGETARIAN
SPRING ROLLS

Squeeze out any excess water from the mushrooms and finely chop, discarding any tough stems. Drain the beanthread noodles and roughly chop.

Heat a wok over a medium–high heat, then add the oil. Toss in the ginger and cook until fragrant. Add the mushrooms and stir for about 2 minutes. Add the carrot, cabbage and spring onions and stir-fry for 1 minute. Add the beanthread noodles and light soy sauce and stir-fry for 1 minute. Add the tofu and cook for a further 1 minute. Season with the salt, pepper and sugar and mix well. Continue cooking for 1–2 minutes, or until the carrot is soft. Remove from the heat and allow to cool.

Place a level tablespoon of the filling towards the bottom of a skin. Roll once to secure the filling, then fold in the sides to create a 10-cm/4-inch width and continue to roll up. Seal with egg white.

Heat a large wok over a high heat. Pour in the oil and heat to 180°C/350°F or until a cube of bread browns in 30 seconds. Without overcrowding the pan, cook the rolls in batches for about 5 minutes, or until golden brown and crispy. Serve with a good soy sauce for dipping.

MAKES 20

6 dried Chinese mushrooms, soaked in warm water for 20 minutes

55 g/2 oz beanthread noodles, soaked in warm water for 20 minutes

2 tbsp vegetable or groundnut oil

1 tbsp finely chopped fresh ginger

100 g/3½ oz carrot, julienned

100 g/3½ oz finely shredded cabbage

1 tbsp finely sliced spring onions

1 tbsp light soy sauce

85 g/3 oz soft tofu, cut into small cubes

½ tsp salt

pinch of white pepper

pinch of sugar

20 spring roll skins

1 egg white, lightly beaten

vegetable or groundnut oil, for deep-frying

soy sauce, to serve

VEGETABLES & SALADS

CLASSIC STIR-FRIED VEGETABLES

Heat a wok over a high heat, then add the oil. Stir-fry three quarters of the chopped spring onions with the garlic and ginger for 30 seconds.

Add the broccoli, pepper and red cabbage and stir-fry for 1–2 minutes. Mix in the baby corn and mushrooms and stir-fry for a further 1–2 minutes.

Finally, add the beansprouts and water chestnuts and cook for 2 minutes. Pour in the soy sauce and stir well.

Serve immediately, garnished with the remaining spring onions.

SERVES 4

3 tbsp sesame oil

8 spring onions, chopped

1 garlic clove, crushed

1 tbsp grated fresh ginger

1 head of broccoli, cut into florets

1 orange or yellow pepper, deseeded and roughly chopped

125 g/4½ oz red cabbage, shredded

125 g/4½ oz baby corn

175 g/6 oz portobello mushrooms, thinly sliced

200 g/7 oz fresh beansprouts

250 g/9 oz canned water chestnuts, drained

4 tsp light soy sauce, or to taste

SPICY FRENCH BEANS

Blanch the beans in a large pan of boiling water for 30 seconds. Drain and set aside.

Heat a wok over a medium–high heat, then add 1 tablespoon of the oil. Stir-fry the beans for about 5 minutes, or until they are beginning to wrinkle. Remove from the wok and set aside.

Add the remaining oil to the wok and stir-fry the chillies and peppers until they are fragrant. Add the garlic, ginger and spring onions and stir-fry until they begin to soften. Add the beans and toss to mix, then add the sea salt and serve immediately.

44

SERVES 4

200 g/7 oz French beans, trimmed and cut diagonally into 3–4 pieces

2 tbsp vegetable or groundnut oil

4 dried chillies, cut into 2–3 pieces

½ tsp Szechuan peppers

1 garlic clove, finely sliced

6 thin slices fresh ginger

2 spring onions, white part only, cut diagonally into thin pieces

pinch of sea salt

STIR-FRIED BROCCOLI

Heat a wok over a medium–high heat, then add the oil. Stir-fry the broccoli for 4–5 minutes.

In a small bowl, combine the soy sauce, cornflour, sugar, ginger, garlic and chilli flakes. Add the mixture to the broccoli. Cook over a low heat, stirring constantly, for 2–3 minutes, until the sauce thickens slightly.

Transfer to a serving dish, garnish with the sesame seeds and serve immediately.

SERVES 4

2 tbsp vegetable oil

2 medium heads of broccoli, cut into florets

2 tbsp light soy sauce

1 tsp cornflour

1 tbsp caster sugar

1 tsp grated fresh ginger

1 garlic clove, crushed

pinch of hot chilli flakes

1 tsp toasted sesame seeds, to garnish

CHUNKY POTATOES WITH CORIANDER LEAVES

Boil the potatoes in a large saucepan of boiling water for 15–25 minutes, or until cooked. Drain, reserving some of the water.

Heat a wok over a medium–high heat, then add plenty of the oil. Cook the potatoes until golden. Drain and set aside.

Heat a clean wok over a medium–high heat, add 1 tablespoon of the oil and stir-fry the pork, pepper and spring onions for 1 minute. Season with the salt, pepper and sugar and stir-fry for a further 1 minute.

Stir in the potato chunks and add the water. Cook for 2–3 minutes, or until the potatoes are warmed through. Turn off the heat, then stir in the coriander and serve warm.

SERVES 6–8

4 potatoes, peeled and cut into large chunks

vegetable or groundnut oil, for frying

100 g/3½ oz pork, not too lean, finely chopped or minced

1 green pepper, deseeded and finely chopped

1 tbsp finely chopped spring onions, white part only

2 tsp salt

½ tsp white pepper

pinch of sugar

2–3 tbsp cooking water from the potatoes

2 tbsp chopped coriander leaves

STIR-FRIED BUTTERNUT SQUASH

Cut the squash in two between the neck and the rounded part. Remove the skin from each piece. Quarter the rounded part and remove the seeds and fibres. Slice lengthways into thin segments. Slice the neck in half lengthways, then crossways into thin semicircles.

Remove and discard the tough stalks from the mushrooms, and thinly slice the caps.

Heat a wok over a medium–high heat, then add the oil. Add half the crushed peppercorns and coriander seeds. Stir for a few seconds, then add the squash in small batches. Fry for 5–7 minutes, carefully turning with tongs, until lightly browned and just tender. Sprinkle with sea salt flakes. Using a slotted spoon, transfer to a large sieve set over a bowl.

Add the mushrooms to the wok and fry for 4–5 minutes, using some of the oil drained from the squash. Add the garlic and lemon zest, and fry for another minute. Sprinkle with sea salt flakes and the rest of the coriander seeds and peppercorns. Add to the squash.

Pour any oil drained from the vegetables into the wok. Stir in the vinegar and stock, and simmer for a few seconds until slightly reduced.

Arrange the spinach on individual serving plates. Pile the vegetables on top, then pour over the juices from the wok. Sprinkle with coriander and serve at once.

SERVES 2

1 butternut squash, weighing about 500 g/18 oz

6 large shiitake mushrooms

5 tbsp rapeseed oil

½ tsp white peppercorns, crushed

½ tsp coriander seeds, crushed

2 large garlic cloves, thinly sliced

finely grated zest of ½ lemon

½ tbsp rice vinegar

4 tbsp chicken or vegetable stock

2 good handfuls of baby spinach, stalks removed

sea salt flakes

chopped fresh coriander, to garnish

STIR-FRIED TOFU WITH BEANSPROUTS

Combine the soy sauce, oyster sauce and chicken stock in a small bowl and set aside.

Heat a wok over a high heat, then add the oil. Heat the oil to 180°C/350°F or until a cube of bread browns in 30 seconds, then add the tofu and fry for 5–7 minutes until golden brown, turning with tongs. Remove with a slotted spoon and drain on kitchen paper. Season with salt and pepper.

Pour the oil from the wok, reserving 1 tablespoon (use the rest in another dish), and wipe out the wok. Heat the reserved oil, add the garlic and stir-fry for a few seconds to flavour the oil. Add the mangetout and spring onions, and stir-fry for 2 minutes.

Add the beansprouts and soy sauce mixture. Stir-fry for 1 minute, then toss in the fried tofu and stir to mix. Sprinkle with the chives and a few drops of sesame oil, and serve at once.

SERVES 2–3

1½ tbsp light soy sauce

1 tbsp oyster sauce

2 tbsp chicken stock or Basic Chinese Stock (see page 8)

groundnut oil, for deep-frying

350 g/12 oz firm tofu, cubed

2 large garlic cloves, thinly sliced

115 g/4 oz mangetout, trimmed and halved diagonally

4 spring onions, sliced diagonally into 2.5-cm/1-inch pieces

115 g/4 oz beansprouts

salt and pepper

½ bunch of garlic chives or ordinary chives, snipped into 2.5-cm/1-inch lengths, to garnish

few drops sesame oil, to garnish

SZECHUAN NUMBING BEEF SALAD

Slice the beef into neat strips measuring about 1 x 4 cm/½ x 1½ inches. Combine the marinade ingredients and pour over the beef. Leave at room temperature for 30 minutes or in the refrigerator for up to 2 days.

Cook the noodles in a saucepan of boiling water for 4 minutes, or according to the instructions on the packet, until soft. Allow to cool. Snip into shorter lengths. Whisk the dressing ingredients until well blended. Combine the noodles, onion, radishes and salad leaves in a large bowl. Whisk the dressing again and pour two thirds of it over the salad. Toss to distribute the noodles, then divide between individual serving plates.

Heat a wok over a medium–high heat, then add the groundnut oil and the Szechuan pepper. Stir for a few seconds to flavour the oil. Add the beef and marinade, and stir-fry for 4–5 minutes until caramelised. Remove with a slotted spoon, and scatter over the salad. Pour over the remaining dressing.

SERVES 4

350 g/12 oz sirloin steak, external fat removed

90 g/3½ oz egg noodles

1 small red onion, halved and thinly sliced into crescents

6 radishes, sliced

4 good handfuls of peppery leaves such as tatsoi, mustard greens and rocket

1½ tbsp groundnut oil

1 tsp Szechuan pepper, crushed

marinade

4 tsp Chinese rice wine or dry sherry

½ tbsp soy sauce

4 tsp sugar

2 tbsp hoisin sauce

2.5-cm/1-inch piece fresh ginger, squeezed in a garlic press

dressing

2 tsp Szechuan pepper, crushed

1½ tbsp light soy sauce

1½ tbsp rice vinegar

2 tbsp cold-pressed sesame oil

PORK & CUCUMBER SALAD

Trim the tenderloin of any sinew and fat, and thinly slice diagonally. Cut each slice in half lengthways. Put in a bowl with the spring onions.

Peel the cucumber, halve lengthways and scoop out the seeds. Thinly slice diagonally and put in a bowl.

Next make the marinade. Using a large mortar and pestle, pound the chopped chillies and the sugar to a watery red paste. Add the fish sauce, lime juice and rice vinegar, stirring to dissolve the sugar. Pour into a measuring jug. Pour one half over the pork and onions, and one half over the cucumber. Leave to marinate for 1 hour, then drain, reserving the marinade.

Put the shredded lettuce, coriander and mint in a bowl, and toss to mix. Divide among individual serving plates. Arrange the cucumber slices on top and dress with the reserved marinade.

Mix the nuts with the lime zest, salt and sugar.

Drain the pork and discard the marinade. Heat a wok over a high heat, then add the oils. Stir-fry the pork for 5 minutes until cooked through and slightly caramelised. Arrange the pork slices on top of the cucumber and sprinkle with the nut mixture. Serve at once.

SERVES 4

450 g/1 lb pork tenderloin

6 spring onions, halved lengthways and sliced into 3

1 ridge cucumber

4 handfuls shredded crisp lettuce

20 g/$\frac{3}{4}$ oz coriander leaves

10 g/$\frac{1}{4}$ oz mint leaves

4 tbsp dry-roasted peanuts, lightly crushed

finely grated zest of 1 lime

1 tsp salt

1 tsp sugar

2 tsp sesame oil

1 tbsp groundnut oil

marinade

2 small red chillies, deseeded and very finely chopped

4 tbsp sugar

3 tbsp Thai fish sauce

4 tbsp lime juice

4 tbsp rice vinegar

CHINESE CHICKEN SALAD

Sprinkle the chicken with the soy sauce and white pepper. Combine the dressing ingredients and whisk to blend.

Heat a wok over a high heat, then add the groundnut oil. Stir-fry the chicken for 4–5 minutes until brown and crisp. Drain on kitchen paper and allow to cool. Wipe out the wok.

Pour enough groundnut oil for deep-frying into the wok. Heat to 180°C/350°F or until a cube of bread browns in 30 seconds, then fry a few noodles at a time until puffed up and crisp. Drain on kitchen paper.

Arrange the Chinese leaves in a shallow serving dish. Place the noodles in a pile on top of the leaves on one side of the dish. Arrange the chicken, spring onion and almonds in the remaining space. Whisk the dressing again and pour over the salad. Dress with the sesame seeds and serve.

SERVES 4

- 3 boneless, skinless chicken breasts, weighing 450 g/1 lb in total, cut into bite-sized pieces
- 2 tsp soy sauce
- ¼ tsp freshly ground white pepper
- 2 tbsp groundnut oil, plus extra for deep-frying
- 50 g/1¾ oz thin rice noodles
- ½ head Chinese leaves, thinly sliced diagonally
- 3 spring onions, green parts included, sliced diagonally
- 40 g/1½ oz almonds with skin, sliced lengthways
- 2 tsp sesame seeds, to garnish

dressing

- 5 tbsp olive oil
- 3 tbsp rice vinegar
- 3 tbsp light soy sauce
- a few drops sesame oil
- salt and pepper

GINGERED
CHICKEN SALAD

VEGETABLES & SALADS

60

Cut the chicken into large cubes, each about 2.5 cm/1 inch.
Mix together the spring onions, ginger, crushed garlic and
2 tablespoons of the oil in a shallow dish and add the chicken.
Cover and marinate for at least 3 hours. Lift the meat out of the
marinade and set aside.

Heat a wok over a high heat, then add the remaining oil. Cook
the onion for 1–2 minutes. Add the garlic, baby corn, mangetout
and pepper and cook for 2–3 minutes, until just tender. Add
the cucumber, half the soy sauce, the sugar and the basil and
mix gently.

Soak the noodles for 2–3 minutes or until tender, and drain
well. Sprinkle the remaining soy sauce over them and arrange on
plates. Top with the cooked vegetables.

Add a little more oil to the wok, if necessary, and cook the
chicken over a fairly high heat until browned on all sides and
cooked through. Arrange the chicken cubes on top of the salad
and serve hot or warm.

SERVES 4

4 skinless, boneless chicken
breasts

4 spring onions, chopped

2.5-cm/1-inch piece fresh ginger,
chopped finely

4 garlic cloves, 2 crushed and
2 chopped

3 tbsp vegetable or groundnut oil

1 onion, sliced

2 garlic cloves, chopped

115 g/4 oz baby corn, halved

115 g/4 oz mangetout, halved
lengthways

1 red pepper, deseeded and sliced

7.5-cm/3-inch piece cucumber,
peeled, deseeded and sliced

4 tbsp Thai soy sauce

1 tbsp soft light brown sugar

few Thai basil leaves

175 g/6 oz fine egg noodles

RICE & TURKEY SALAD

Set aside 3 tablespoons of the chicken stock and bring the remainder to the boil in a large saucepan. Add the rice and cook for 30 minutes or until tender. Drain and cool slightly.

Heat a wok over a high heat, then add 1 tablespoon of the oil. Stir-fry the turkey over medium heat for 3–4 minutes or until cooked through. Using a slotted spoon, transfer the turkey to a dish. Add the mangetout and mushrooms to the wok and stir-fry for 1 minute. Add the reserved stock, bring to the boil, then reduce the heat, cover and simmer for 3–4 minutes. Transfer the vegetables to the dish and cool slightly.

Thoroughly mix together the rice, turkey, mangetout, mushrooms, nuts, coriander and garlic chives, then season to taste with salt and pepper. Drizzle with the remaining corn oil and the vinegar and garnish with fresh garlic chives. Serve warm.

SERVES 4

1 litre/1¾ pints chicken stock

200 g/7 oz mixed long-grain and wild rice

2 tbsp corn oil

225 g/8 oz skinless, boneless turkey breast, trimmed of all visible fat and cut into thin strips

115 g/4 oz mangetout

115 g/4 oz oyster mushrooms, torn into pieces

25 g/1 oz shelled pistachio nuts, finely chopped

2 tbsp chopped fresh coriander

1 tbsp snipped fresh garlic chives

salt and pepper

1 tbsp balsamic vinegar

fresh garlic chives, to garnish

DUCK SALAD

Unwrap the duck and let the skin dry out overnight in the refrigerator.

The following day, slash the skin side 5–6 times. Mix together the lemon grass, 2 tablespoons of the vegetable oil, all the sesame oil, fish sauce, chilli and curry paste in a shallow dish and place the duck breasts in the mixture. Turn to coat and to rub the marinade into the meat. Chill for 2–3 hours.

Heat a wok over a medium–high heat, then add the remaining oil. Cook the duck skin-side down, over a medium heat, for 3–4 minutes until the skin is browned and crisp and the meat is cooked most of the way through.

Turn the breasts over and cook until browned and the meat is cooked to your liking.

Meanwhile, arrange the pineapple, cucumber, tomatoes, and onion on a platter. Mix together the dressing ingredients and pour over the top.

Lift the duck out of the wok and slice thickly. Arrange the duck slices on top of the salad and serve while still hot.

SERVES 4

4 boneless duck breasts, skin on

1 lemon grass stem, broken into three and each cut in half lengthways

3 tbsp vegetable or groundnut oil

2 tbsp sesame oil

1 tsp Thai fish sauce

1 fresh green chilli, deseeded and chopped

2 tbsp Thai red curry paste

½ fresh pineapple, peeled and sliced

7.5-cm/3-inch piece cucumber, peeled, deseeded and sliced

3 tomatoes, cut into wedges

1 onion, sliced thinly

dressing

juice of 1 lemon

2 garlic cloves, crushed

1 tsp jaggery

2 tbsp vegetable or groundnut oil

CHINESE PRAWN SALAD

Cook the noodles in a saucepan of boiling water for 4 minutes, or according to the instructions on the packet, until soft. Drain thoroughly and pat dry with kitchen paper.

Heat a wok over a high heat, then add the sunflower oil. Add the noodles and stir-fry for 5 minutes, tossing frequently.

Remove the wok from the heat and add the sesame oil, sesame seeds and beansprouts, tossing to mix well.

Mix together the mango, spring onions, radishes, prawns, soy sauce and sherry in a separate bowl. Toss the prawn mixture with the noodles. Alternatively, arrange the noodles around the edge of a serving plate and pile the prawn mixture into the centre. Serve immediately.

SERVES 4

250 g/9 oz thin egg noodles

3 tbsp sunflower oil

1 tbsp sesame oil

1 tbsp sesame seeds

175 g/6 oz fresh beansprouts

1 mango, peeled, pitted and sliced

6 spring onions, sliced

75 g/2¾ oz radishes, sliced

350 g/12 oz cooked peeled prawns

2 tbsp light soy sauce

1 tbsp sherry

CARAMELISED TUNA SALAD

To make the dressing, heat a small wok over high heat. Add the oil and fry the ginger and chilli for a few seconds. Add the soy sauce, fish sauce and tamarind paste. Stir for 30 seconds, then add the sugar and stir until dissolved. Remove the wok from the heat and set aside.

Rinse the beansprouts in boiling water and drain. Blot dry with kitchen paper. Peel the cucumber, halve lengthways and scoop out the seeds. Thinly slice the flesh diagonally.

Put the beansprouts, cucumber, coriander and mint leaves in a bowl. Season with a pinch of salt and a few drops of toasted sesame oil. Toss to combine, then divide between individual serving plates.

Heat a wok over a high heat, then add the groundnut and sesame oils. Quickly stir-fry the tuna, turning with tongs, until coloured on the outside but still slightly red in the middle. Arrange the tuna chunks on top of the salad.

Reheat the dressing, thinning with a spoonful of water if necessary, and pour over the tuna. Sprinkle with the crushed peanuts and serve at once.

SERVES 4

175 g/6 oz fresh beansprouts

10 cm/4 inch piece of cucumber

20 g/¾ oz coriander leaves

20 g/¾ oz mint leaves

1 tsp sesame oil, plus a few drops for drizzling

1 tbsp groundnut oil

450 g/1 lb fresh tuna, cut into 2.5-cm/1-inch chunks

salt

2 tbsp salted roasted peanuts, crushed, to garnish

dressing

2 tsp rapeseed oil

1 tsp finely chopped fresh ginger

½–1 small red chilli, deseeded and finely chopped

4 tbsp light soy sauce

1 tbsp Thai fish sauce

1 tbsp tamarind paste

6 tbsp soft brown sugar

MEAT

BEEF CHOW MEIN

Combine all the marinade ingredients in a bowl and marinate the beef for at least 20 minutes.

Cook the noodles in a saucepan of boiling water for 4 minutes, or according to the instructions on the packet, until soft. Drain, then rinse under cold running water and set aside.

Heat a wok over a medium–high heat, then add the oil. Stir-fry the beef for about 1 minute, until the meat has changed colour, then add the onion and cook for 1 minute, then add the green pepper and beansprouts. Cook until any water from the vegetables has evaporated.

Add the salt, sugar, rice wine and soy sauces. Stir in the noodles and toss for 1 minute. Finally, stir in the spring onion and serve.

SERVES 4

280 g/10 oz fillet steak, cut into thin strips

225 g/8 oz medium egg noodles

2 tbsp vegetable or groundnut oil

1 onion, finely sliced

1 green pepper, deseeded and finely sliced

140 g/5 oz fresh beansprouts

1 tsp salt

pinch of sugar

2 tsp Chinese rice wine

2 tbsp light soy sauce

1 tbsp dark soy sauce

1 tbsp finely shredded spring onion

marinade

1 tsp light soy sauce

dash of sesame oil

½ tsp Chinese rice wine

pinch of white pepper

HOT SESAME BEEF

Mix the beef with 1 tablespoon of the sesame seeds in a small bowl. In a separate bowl, whisk together the stock, soy sauce, ginger, garlic, cornflour and chilli flakes.

Heat a wok over a medium–high heat, then add 2 tablespoons of the sesame oil. Stir-fry the beef for 2–3 minutes. Remove and set aside.

Discard any oil left in the wok, then wipe with kitchen paper to remove any stray sesame seeds. Heat the remaining oil in the wok, add the broccoli, orange pepper, chilli and chilli oil, and stir-fry for 2–3 minutes. Stir in the stock mixture, cover and simmer for 2 minutes.

Return the beef to the wok and simmer until the juices thicken, stirring occasionally. Cook for a futher 1–2 minutes.

Sprinkle with the remaining sesame seeds. Serve garnished with chopped coriander.

SERVES 4

500 g/1 lb 2 oz beef fillet, cut into thin strips

1½ tbsp sesame seeds

125 ml/4 fl oz beef stock

2 tbsp light soy sauce

2 tbsp grated fresh ginger

2 garlic cloves, finely chopped

1 tsp cornflour

½ tsp chilli flakes

3 tbsp sesame oil

1 large head of broccoli, cut into florets

1 orange pepper, deseeded and thinly sliced

1 fresh red chilli, deseeded and finely sliced

1 tbsp chilli oil, or to taste

1 tbsp chopped fresh coriander, to garnish

BEEF WITH BLACK PEPPER & LIME

Pound the steak with the blunt side of a knife. Slice diagonally across the grain into thin bite-sized pieces and put in a shallow bowl.

Combine the sugar, peppercorns, soy sauce, chilli, garlic and half the lime juice in a bowl, mixing well. Pour over the beef, stirring to coat. Leave to marinate for 1 hour at room temperature, or overnight in the refrigerator.

Arrange the Chinese leaves in a shallow serving dish. Scatter with the red onion slices.

Heat a wok over a high heat, then add the oil. Stir-fry the meat for 3 minutes. Add the fish sauce and the remaining lime juice, and stir-fry for a further minute.

Tip the beef and juices over the Chinese leaves and onion, then scatter over the mint. Garnish with lime wedges and serve immediately with rice.

SERVES 2–3

350 g/12 oz skirt steak

½ tbsp palm sugar or light brown sugar

1 tbsp black peppercorns, crushed

4 tsp soy sauce

1 fresh red bird's eye chilli, deseeded and finely chopped

½ head of garlic, divided into cloves and crushed

2 tbsp lime juice

½ head Chinese leaves, sliced

½ red onion, thinly sliced

1½ tbsp groundnut oil

½ tsp Thai fish sauce

3 tbsp chopped fresh mint

lime wedges, to garnish

freshly cooked plain rice, to serve

BEEF & BOK CHOI STIR-FRY

Pound the steak with the blunt side of a knife. Slice diagonally across the grain into thin bite-sized pieces and put in a shallow bowl.

Combine the marinade ingredients in a bowl and pour over the beef, stirring to coat. Leave to marinate for 1 hour at room temperature, or overnight in the refrigerator.

Heat a wok over a medium–high heat, then add the oil. Stir-fry the shallot, ginger and chilli for 1 minute. Increase the heat to high and add the beef and marinade. Stir-fry for 3 minutes. Add the bok choi stalks and stir-fry for 1 minute. Add the leaves and stir-fry for a further minute.

Mix the cornflour and stock to a smooth paste. Add to the wok and stir-fry for 1 minute, until slightly thickened. Transfer to a warmed serving dish and sprinkle with the coriander. Serve immediately.

SERVES 2–3

350 g/12 oz skirt steak

2 tbsp groundnut oil

1 shallot, chopped

2 tsp finely chopped fresh ginger

1 fresh red chilli, deseeded and thinly sliced

350 g/12 oz bok choi, stalks cut into 2.5-cm/1-inch squares and leaves sliced into wide ribbons

1 tbsp cornflour

2 tbsp beef stock or water

3 tbsp chopped fresh coriander

marinade

2 tbsp soy sauce

$1\frac{1}{2}$ tbsp Chinese rice wine or dry sherry

$\frac{1}{2}$ tsp sugar

$\frac{1}{2}$ tsp pepper

$\frac{1}{4}$ tsp salt

BEEF WITH MIXED MUSHROOMS

Grind the Szechuan peppers with the salt, using a mortar and pestle. Sprinkle over both sides of the meat, pressing in well. Slice the meat diagonally across the grain into thin bite-sized pieces and set aside.

Rinse the mushrooms and dry with kitchen paper. If using clumping mushrooms, such as enoki and buna shimeji, slice off the root and separate the clump. Slice cremini mushrooms in half.

Mix the cornflour to a paste with 2 tablespoons of the stock. Add the rice wine and soy sauce, mixing well.

Heat a wok over a medium–high heat, then add 1 tablespoon of the oil. Fry the shallot and ginger for 1 minute. Add the garlic and fry for a few seconds, then add the mushrooms and 2 tablespoons of the stock. Stir-fry for 4 minutes. Add the cornflour mixture and the remaining stock. Bring to the boil, stirring, then reduce the heat and simmer for 2 minutes. Transfer to a warmed serving dish.

Clean the wok and heat over a high heat. Add the remaining oil. Add the beef and stir-fry for 3 minutes. Add to the mushroom mixture and sprinkle with the coriander. Serve immediately.

SERVES 2–3

1½ tbsp Szechuan peppers

½ tsp salt

350 g/12 oz sirloin or rump steak

200 g/7 oz mixed small mushrooms, such as cremini, enoki and buna shimeji

½ tbsp cornflour

125 ml/4 fl oz Spicy Beef Stock (see page 8) or beef stock

2 tsp Chinese rice wine or dry sherry

4 tsp soy sauce

3 tbsp groundnut oil

1 shallot, finely chopped

1 tsp finely chopped fresh ginger

1 large garlic clove, thinly sliced

3 tbsp chopped fresh coriander, to garnish

PAD THAI

Soak the noodles in enough lukewarm water to cover for
15 minutes, or cook according to the instructions on the packet,
until soft. Drain well and set aside.

Heat a wok over a medium–high heat, then add the oil. Stir-fry
the garlic, chillies and pork for 2–3 minutes. Add the prawns and
stir-fry for a further 2–3 minutes.

Add the chives and noodles, then cover and cook for
1–2 minutes. Add the fish sauce, lime juice, sugar and eggs.
Cook, stirring and tossing constantly to mix in the eggs.

Stir in the beansprouts, coriander and peanuts and mix well,
then transfer to serving dishes. Scatter over some extra peanuts
and serve immediately, garnished with coriander sprigs.

SERVES 4

225 g/8 oz thick rice noodles

2 tbsp vegetable or groundnut oil

2 garlic cloves, chopped

2 fresh red chillies, deseeded and
chopped

175 g/6 oz pork fillet, thinly sliced

115 g/4 oz raw prawns, peeled,
deveined and chopped

8 fresh Chinese chives, snipped

2 tbsp Thai fish sauce

juice of 1 lime

2 tsp palm sugar or light brown
sugar

2 eggs, beaten

115 g/4 oz fresh beansprouts

4 tbsp chopped fresh coriander,
plus extra sprigs to garnish

115 g/4 oz unsalted peanuts,
chopped, plus extra to serve

PORK STIR FRY WITH CASHEWS, LIME & MINT

Diagonally slice the pork across the grain into thin bite-sized pieces. Flatten with the back of a knife blade and spread out on a plate. Using a mortar and pestle, crush the coriander seeds, peppercorns, salt, sugar and lime rind together. Spread the mixture over both sides of the pork, pressing it in well. Leave to stand for 15 minutes.

Heat a wok over a high heat, then add 1 tablespoon of the oil. Stir-fry the pork for 2–3 minutes, until no longer pink. Transfer to a plate with the juices. Wipe the wok clean with kitchen paper.

Heat the wok over a medium–high heat, then add the remaining oil. Stir-fry the ginger and garlic for a few seconds. Add the white spring onion and green pepper, and stir-fry for 2 minutes. Add the cashew nuts and salt, then stir-fry for a further minute.

Increase the heat to high, then return the pork and juices to the wok. Add the stock, lime juice, fish sauce and the green spring onion. Stir-fry for 30 seconds to heat through, then sprinkle with the mint and serve.

SERVES 2

280 g/10 oz pork fillet

1 tsp coriander seeds

½ tsp white peppercorns

¼ tsp salt

¼ tsp sugar

juice and finely grated rind of 1 lime

2 tbsp groundnut oil

1 tsp finely chopped fresh ginger

1 garlic clove, thinly sliced

3 spring onions, white and green parts separated, then halved lengthways and sliced into 2-cm/¾-inch pieces

1 small green pepper, deseeded and thinly sliced

2 tbsp cashew nuts, roughly chopped

large pinch of salt

1 tbsp chicken stock

1 tsp Thai fish sauce

2 tbsp roughly chopped fresh mint, to garnish

PORK BELLY ON CHINESE LEAVES

Using the tip of a very sharp knife, score the pork rind at
1-cm/½-inch intervals. Combine the marinade ingredients, pour
the mixture into a dish and add the pork, rubbing the marinade
into the slashes. Leave to stand at room temperature for 1 hour,
turning occasionally.

Preheat the oven to 220°C/425°F/Gas Mark 7. Line a small
roasting tin with foil and put a rack in it. Reserving the marinade,
place the pork on the rack and put the tin on the top shelf of the
oven. Roast for 15 minutes, then reduce the oven temperature
to 180°C/350°F/Gas Mark 4. Turn the pork over and brush with
the marinade. Roast for 20 minutes, then turn, brush with the
marinade again and roast for a further 20 minutes. Remove
from the oven and leave to cool. Diagonally slice the pork
into 1-cm/½-inch pieces. Put in a bowl and mix with the
remaining marinade.

Heat a wok over a high heat, then add 1 tablespoon of the oil.
Add the pork slices and marinade, and stir-fry for 2 minutes,
until the marinade is reduced and bubbling. Pour in the stock,
scraping up any sediment. Stir-fry for 2 minutes, until reduced.
Remove from the wok and keep warm. Wipe the wok clean with
kitchen paper.

Heat the wok over a high heat, then add the remaining oil. Add
the ginger and stir-fry for a few seconds. Add the Chinese leaves,
spring onions, sugar and salt, and stir-fry for 1 minute. Transfer
the vegetables to a warmed serving dish. Pour the pork and
juices over the top and serve immediately.

SERVES 2

4 strips boneless pork belly, about
650 g/1 lb 7 oz in total

2 tbsp groundnut oil

6 tbsp Basic Chinese Stock
(see page 8) or chicken stock

1 thin slice fresh ginger

½ head Chinese leaves, sliced
diagonally into ribbons

6 spring onions, green parts
included, sliced diagonally into
4-cm/1½-inch pieces

½ tsp sugar

¼ tsp salt

marinade

2 tbsp sugar

2 tbsp Chinese rice wine or dry
sherry

1 tbsp soy sauce

4-cm/1½-inch piece fresh ginger,
roughly chopped and squeezed
in a garlic press

½ tsp salt

¼ tsp Chinese five-spice

4 tbsp hoisin sauce

PORK, CARROT & GINGER STIR FRY

Diagonally slice the pork across the grain very thinly, then cut into 4-cm/1½-inch lengths. Put in a bowl. Combine the marinade ingredients and pour over the pork. Leave to stand for 30 minutes.

Heat a wok over a medium heat, then add the oil. Stir-fry the garlic and chilli for 30 seconds, or until the garlic just starts to colour.

Add the pork and marinade, and increase the heat to high. Stir-fry for 1 minute, then add the carrots, ginger, bamboo shoots and Szechuan peppers. Stir-fry for a further minute, then pour in the stock and soy sauce. Stir-fry for 4–5 minutes, until the sauce has reduced slightly. Transfer to a warmed dish and serve immediately.

SERVES 2

250 g/9 oz pork fillet

2 tbsp groundnut oil

2 large garlic cloves, thinly sliced

1 fresh green chilli, deseeded and thinly sliced diagonally

6 carrots, cut into thin strips

50 g/1¾ oz fresh ginger, cut into thin strips

140 g/5 oz canned bamboo shoots, drained

1½ tsp Szechuan peppers, crushed

100 ml/3½ fl oz Basic Chinese Stock (see page 8) or chicken stock

2 tbsp light soy sauce

marinade

2 tsp Chinese rice wine or dry sherry

2 tsp light soy sauce

½ tsp sugar

¼ tsp salt

JAPANESE-STYLE PORK

Diagonally slice the pork across the grain very thinly, then cut into 4-cm/1½-inch lengths. Put in a bowl. Combine the marinade ingredients, stirring well to mix in the honey, and pour over the pork. Leave to stand for 1 hour at room temperature, or overnight in the refrigerator. Drain the pork in a sieve set over a bowl, reserving the marinade.

Heat a wok over a medium heat, then add the groundnut oil. Stir-fry the garlic for a few seconds, then add the beans and stir-fry for 1 minute. Add the pork and marinade, and increase the heat to high. Season to taste with salt and pepper, and stir-fry for 4–5 minutes, or until the beans are tender and the pork is cooked through.

Sprinkle with the sesame seeds pour in the oil, then fry for a further 30 seconds. Transfer to a warmed serving dish and serve immediately.

SERVES 2

280 g/10 oz pork fillet

2 tbsp groundnut oil

1 garlic clove, thinly sliced

115 g/4 oz French beans, trimmed and sliced into 4-cm/1½-inch lengths

1½ tsp sesame seeds

½ tsp sesame oil

salt and pepper

marinade

3 tbsp shoyu or tamari (Japanese soy sauce)

3 tbsp mirin

finely grated rind and juice of ½ orange

1 tbsp clear honey

½ –1 fresh red chilli, deseeded and finely chopped

1 tsp finely chopped fresh ginger

¼ tsp salt

STIR-FRIED LAMB WITH ORANGE

Heat a wok, without adding any oil. Add the lamb mince and dry-fry for 5 minutes, or until evenly browned. Drain away any excess fat from the wok.

Add the garlic, cumin seeds, coriander and red onion to the wok and stir-fry for a further 5 minutes.

Stir in the orange rind and juice and the soy sauce, mixing until thoroughly combined. Cover, reduce the heat and leave to simmer, stirring occasionally, for 15 minutes.

Remove the lid, increase the heat and add the orange segments. Stir to mix.

Season to taste with salt and pepper and heat through for a further 2–3 minutes. Transfer the stir-fry to warmed serving dishes and garnish with snipped chives and strips of orange zest. Serve immediately.

SERVES 4

450 g/1 lb fresh lamb mince

2 garlic cloves, crushed

1 tsp cumin seeds

1 tsp ground coriander

1 red onion, sliced

finely grated rind and juice of
   1 orange

2 tbsp soy sauce

1 orange, peeled and segmented

salt and pepper

snipped fresh chives and strips of
   orange zest, to garnish

LAMB WITH BLACK BEAN SAUCE

Using a sharp knife, slice the lamb into very thin strips.

Mix together the egg white, cornflour and Chinese five-spice. Toss the lamb strips in the mixture until evenly coated.

Heat a wok over a high heat, then add the oil. Stir-fry the lamb for 5 minutes, or until it crispens around the edges.

Add the onion and pepper slices to the wok and stir-fry for 5–6 minutes, or until the vegetables just begin to soften.

Stir the black bean sauce into the mixture in the wok and heat through.

Transfer the lamb and sauce to warmed serving dishes and serve with cooked noodles.

SERVES 4

450 g/1 lb lamb neck fillet or boneless leg of lamb

1 egg white, lightly beaten

4 tbsp cornflour

1 tsp Chinese five-spice

3 tbsp sunflower oil

1 red onion, sliced

1 red pepper, deseeded and sliced

1 green pepper, deseeded and sliced

1 yellow or orange pepper, deseeded and sliced

5 tbsp black bean sauce

freshly cooked noodles, to serve

LAMB & LEEK
STIR FRY

Diagonally slice the lamb across the grain into thin bite-sized pieces. Flatten with the back of a knife blade and put in a bowl. Combine the garlic, soy sauce, rice wine, sugar and salt. Pour the mixture over the lamb. Leave to stand for 1 hour at room temperature, or overnight in the refrigerator.

   Mix the cornflour to a thin paste with the stock. Heat a wok over a high heat, then add 1 tablespoon of the oil. Add the lamb and stir-fry for 1 minute, then season to taste with pepper. Add the cornflour paste and stir-fry for a further minute. Remove from the wok and keep warm. Wipe the wok clean with kitchen paper.

   Heat the wok over a high heat, the add the remaining oil. Add the leeks and chicken stock, and stir-fry for 2 minutes, until just cooked and still bright green and crisp. Return the lamb to the wok and stir-fry for 30 seconds. Transfer to a warmed serving dish and serve immediately.

SERVES 2

280 g/10 oz lamb neck fillet

1 garlic clove, finely chopped

2 tsp soy sauce

2 tsp Chinese rice wine or dry
   sherry

1/2 tsp sugar

1/4 tsp salt

1/2 tbsp cornflour

Basic Chinese Stock (see page 8)
   or chicken stock

2 tbsp groundnut oil

3 leeks, green part included,
   sliced into 4-cm/1 1/2-inch pieces

1 tbsp chicken stock or water

pepper

LAMB WITH
LIME LEAVES

Using a sharp knife, cut the lamb into thin strips or cubes.
Heat a wok over a high heat, then add the oil. Add the chillies,
garlic, shallots, lemon grass, kaffir lime leaves, tamarind paste
and sugar.

Add the lamb to the wok and stir-fry for 5 minutes, tossing well
so that the lamb is evenly coated in the spice mixture.

Pour the coconut milk into the wok and bring to the boil.
Reduce the heat and simmer for 20 minutes.

Add the cherry tomatoes and chopped coriander to the wok
and simmer for 5 minutes. Transfer to serving plates and serve
with rice.

SERVES 4

450 g/1 lb lean boneless lamb
 (leg or loin fillet)

2 tbsp groundnut oil

2 fresh bird's eye chillies,
 deseeded and finely chopped

2 garlic cloves, crushed

4 shallots, chopped

2 lemon grass stems, sliced

6 fresh kaffir lime leaves

1 tbsp tamarind paste

2 tbsp palm sugar or light brown
 sugar

300 ml/10 fl oz coconut milk

175 g/6 oz cherry tomatoes,
 halved

1 tbsp chopped fresh coriander

freshly cooked Thai fragrant rice,
 to serve

POULTRY

SWEET & SOUR CHICKEN

Combine all the marinade ingredients in a bowl and marinate the chicken for at least 20 minutes.

To prepare the sauce, heat the vinegar in a pan and add the sugar, soy sauce and tomato ketchup. Stir to dissolve the sugar, then set aside.

Heat a wok over a high heat, then add 3 tablespoons of the vegetable oil. Stir-fry the chicken until it starts to turn golden brown. Remove and set aside. Wipe the wok clean with kitchen paper.

Heat the wok over a high heat, and add the remaining vegetable oil and cook the garlic and ginger until fragrant. Add the vegetables and cook for 2 minutes. Add the chicken and cook for 1 minute. Finally, add the sauce and the sesame oil, then stir in the spring onion and serve immediately with rice.

SERVES 4–6

450 g/1 lb lean chicken, cubed

5 tbsp vegetable or groundnut oil

½ tsp crushed garlic

½ tsp finely chopped fresh ginger

1 green pepper, deseeded and roughly chopped

1 onion, roughly chopped

1 carrot, finely sliced

1 tsp sesame oil

1 tbsp finely chopped spring onion

freshly cooked plain rice, to serve

marinade

2 tsp light soy sauce

1 tsp Chinese rice wine

pinch of white pepper

½ tsp salt

dash of sesame oil

sauce

8 tbsp rice vinegar

4 tbsp sugar

2 tsp light soy sauce

6 tbsp tomato ketchup

GONG BAU CHICKEN

Combine all the marinade ingredients in a bowl and marinate the chicken, covered, for at least 20 minutes. Combine all the ingredients for the sauce and set aside.

Heat a wok over a high heat, then add the vegetable oil. Stir-fry the chillies and peppers until crisp and fragrant. Toss in the chicken pieces. When they begin to turn white, add the garlic, ginger and spring onion. Stir-fry for about 5 minutes, or until the chicken is cooked through.

Pour in the sauce and mix together thoroughly, then stir in the peanuts. Serve immediately with rice.

SERVES 4

2 skinless, boneless chicken breasts, cut into cubes

1 tbsp vegetable or groundnut oil

10 dried red chillies, or to taste, each snipped into 2–3 pieces

1 tsp Szechuan peppers

3 garlic cloves, finely sliced

2.5-cm/1-inch piece fresh ginger, finely sliced

1 tbsp finely chopped spring onion

85 g/3 oz roasted peanuts

freshly cooked plain rice, to serve

marinade

2 tsp light soy sauce

1 tsp Chinese rice wine

½ tsp sugar

sauce

1 tsp light soy sauce

1 tsp dark soy sauce

1 tsp black rice vinegar

a few drops of sesame oil

2 tbsp chicken stock

1 tsp sugar

CHICKEN WITH CASHEW NUTS

Combine all the marinade ingredients in a bowl and marinate the chicken for at least 20 minutes.

Squeeze any excess water from the mushrooms and finely slice, discarding any tough stems. Reserve the soaking water.

Heat a wok over a medium–high heat, then add 1 tablespoon of the oil. Add the ginger and stir-fry until fragrant. Stir in the chicken and cook for 2 minutes, or until it begins to turn brown. Before the chicken is cooked through, remove and set aside. Wipe the wok clean with kitchen paper.

Heat the wok over a medium–high heat, then add the remaining oil. Stir-fry the garlic until fragrant. Add the mushrooms and red pepper and stir-fry for 1 minute. Add about 2 tablespoons of the mushroom-soaking water and cook for about 2 minutes, or until the water has evaporated.

Return the chicken to the wok, then add the soy sauce and cashew nuts and stir-fry for 2 minutes, or until the chicken is cooked through.

SERVES 4–6

450 g/1 lb skinless, boneless chicken breasts, cut into bite-sized pieces

2 dried Chinese mushrooms, soaked in warm water for 20 minutes

2 tbsp vegetable or groundnut oil

4 slices fresh ginger

1 tsp finely chopped garlic

1 red pepper, deseeded and cut into 2.5-cm/1-inch squares

1 tbsp light soy sauce

85 g/3 oz roasted cashew nuts

marinade

1 tsp Chinese rice wine

pinch of sugar

$\frac{1}{2}$ tsp salt

2 tbsp light soy sauce

CHICKEN CHOW MEIN

Cook the noodles in a saucepan of boiling water for 4 minutes, or according to the instructions on the packet, until soft. Drain and set aside.

Heat a wok over a medium heat, then add the sunflower oil. Add the chicken, garlic, red pepper, mushrooms, spring onions and beansprouts to the wok and stir-fry for about 5 minutes.

Add the noodles to the wok, toss well and stir-fry for a further 5 minutes. Drizzle over the soy sauce and sesame oil and toss until thoroughly combined.

Transfer to warmed serving dishes and serve immediately.

SERVES 4

250 g/9 oz medium egg noodles

2 tbsp sunflower oil

280 g/10 oz cooked chicken breasts, shredded

1 garlic clove, finely chopped

1 red pepper, deseeded and thinly sliced

100 g/3½ oz shiitake mushrooms, sliced

6 spring onions, sliced

100 g/3½ oz fresh beansprouts

3 tbsp soy sauce

1 tbsp sesame oil

THAI GREEN CHICKEN CURRY

Heat a wok over a medium–high heat, then add the oil. Stir-fry the onion and garlic for 1–2 minutes, until starting to soften. Add the curry paste and stir-fry for 1–2 minutes.

Add the coconut milk, stock and lime leaves, bring to the boil and add the chicken. Reduce the heat and simmer gently for 15–20 minutes, until the chicken is tender.

Add the fish sauce, soy sauce, lime rind and juice and sugar. Cook for 2–3 minutes, until the sugar has dissolved. Garnish with chopped coriander and serve immediately with rice.

SERVES 4

1 tbsp vegetable or groundnut oil

1 onion, sliced

1 garlic clove, finely chopped

2–3 tbsp Thai green curry paste

400 ml/14 fl oz coconut milk

150 ml/5 fl oz chicken stock

4 kaffir lime leaves

4 skinless, boneless chicken breasts, cut into cubes

1 tbsp Thai fish sauce

2 tbsp Thai soy sauce

grated rind and juice of ½ lime

1 tsp soft light brown sugar

4 tbsp chopped fresh coriander, to garnish

freshly cooked jasmine rice, to serve

THAI RED CHICKEN CURRY

Place the garlic, chillies, lemon grass, lime rind, lime leaves, curry paste and coriander seeds in a food processor and process until the mixture is smooth.

Heat a wok over a medium–high heat, then add the oil. Add the chicken and the garlic mixture and stir-fry for 5 minutes. Add the coconut milk, stock and soy sauce and bring to the boil. Reduce the heat and cook, stirring, for a further 3 minutes. Stir in the ground peanuts and simmer for 20 minutes.

Add the spring onions, red pepper and aubergines and simmer, stirring occasionally, for a further 10 minutes. Remove from the heat and stir in the coriander. Serve immediately with jasmine rice, garnished with extra coriander.

SERVES 4

6 garlic cloves, chopped

2 fresh red chillies, chopped

2 tbsp chopped fresh lemon grass

1 tsp finely grated lime rind

1 tbsp chopped fresh kaffir lime leaves

1 tbsp Thai red curry paste

1 tbsp coriander seeds, toasted and crushed

1 tbsp chilli oil

4 skinless, boneless chicken breasts, sliced

300 ml/10 fl oz coconut milk

300 ml/10 fl oz chicken stock

1 tbsp soy sauce

55 g/2 oz unsalted peanuts, toasted and ground

3 spring onions, diagonally sliced

1 red pepper, deseeded and sliced

3 Thai aubergines, sliced

2 tbsp chopped fresh coriander, plus extra to garnish

freshly cooked jasmine rice, to serve

PEPPERED CHICKEN STIR FRY

In a small bowl, combine half the soy sauce, the cornflour, rice wine and salt.

Put the chicken pieces in a shallow dish and pour over the soy sauce mixture, stirring to coat. Leave to stand for 15 minutes.

Mix the remaining soy sauce with the stock and oyster sauce, and set aside.

Heat a wok over a high heat, then add the oil. Add the chicken and stir-fry for 3 minutes, until no longer pink. Remove from the wok with a slotted spoon and drain on kitchen paper.

Reduce the heat slightly, then add the ginger, garlic, white spring onion and the crushed peppercorns, and stir for a few seconds. Add the baby corn, red pepper and water chestnuts. Stir-fry for 2 minutes, then return the chicken to the wok. Add the mangetout and the soy sauce mixture, and stir-fry for 1–2 minutes, until the sauce is thickened.

Sprinkle with the sliced green spring onion and cook for a few more seconds. Serve immediately.

SERVES 4–6

4 tsp soy sauce

1 tbsp cornflour

1 tbsp Chinese rice wine or dry sherry

¼ tsp salt

350 g/12 oz skinless, boneless chicken breasts, cut into cubes

6 tbsp Basic Chinese Stock (see page 8) or chicken stock

1 tbsp oyster sauce

4 tbsp groundnut oil

1 tsp finely chopped fresh ginger

1 large garlic clove, thinly sliced

4 spring onions, white and green parts separated, diagonally sliced into 2-cm/¾-inch pieces

½ tbsp white peppercorns, crushed

8 baby corn, halved diagonally

½ small red pepper, deseeded and thinly sliced

140 g/5 oz canned water chestnuts, drained

115 g/4 oz mangetout, halved diagonally

YAKI SOBA

Cook the noodles according to the instructions on the packet. Drain well, and tip into a bowl.

Mix the onion, beansprouts, red pepper, chicken and prawns together in a separate bowl. Stir through the noodles.

Heat a wok over a high heat, then add the groundnut oil. Add the noodle mixture and stir-fry for 4 minutes, or until golden, then add the shoyu, mirin and sesame oil and toss together.

Divide the mixture between 2 bowls, sprinkle with the sesame seeds and spring onions and serve immediately.

SERVES 2

400 g/14 oz ramen noodles

1 onion, finely sliced

200 g/7 oz fresh beansprouts

1 red pepper, deseeded and thinly sliced

1 boneless, skin-on cooked chicken breast, about 150 g/ 5½ oz, sliced

12 cooked peeled prawns

1 tbsp groundnut oil

2 tbsp shoyu (Japanese soy sauce)

½ tbsp mirin

1 tsp sesame oil

1 tsp toasted sesame seeds

2 spring onions, finely sliced

TURKEY TERIYAKI

Mix the glaze ingredients in a small saucepan over a low–medium heat. Stir until the honey has melted, then remove from the heat and leave to cool.

Put the turkey in a large shallow dish. Pour over the glaze, turning the strips so they are well coated. Leave to marinate for 30 minutes at room temperature, or overnight in the refrigerator.

Using a slotted spoon, remove the turkey from the marinade, shaking off the excess liquid. Reserve the marinade.

Heat a wok over a medium–high heat, then add the oil. Add the turkey and stir-fry for 2 minutes. Add the yellow pepper and spring onions, and fry for 1 minute. Pour in the reserved marinade. Bring to the boil, then reduce the heat slightly and cook for 3–4 minutes, until the turkey is cooked through.

Transfer the turkey and vegetables to a warmed serving dish. Boil the liquid remaining in the wok until syrupy, then pour over the turkey. Serve immediately with rice.

SERVES 4

450 g/1 lb turkey steaks, cut into strips

3 tbsp groundnut oil

1 small yellow pepper, deseeded and sliced into thin strips

8 spring onions, green part included, diagonally sliced into 2.5-cm/1-inch pieces

freshly cooked plain rice, to serve

teriyaki glaze

5 tbsp shoyu (Japanese soy sauce)

5 tbsp mirin

2 tbsp clear honey

1 tsp finely chopped fresh ginger

TURKEY WITH BOK CHOI & MUSHROOMS

Cook the noodles in a saucepan of boiling water for 4 minutes, or according to the instructions on the packet, until soft. Drain, rinse and drain again, then leave to cool.

Heat a wok over a medium–high heat, then add the oil. Stir-fry the garlic and ginger for a few seconds to flavour the oil.

Add the turkey and stir-fry for 2 minutes, until no longer pink. Add the mushrooms and bok choi stalks, and stir-fry for 2 minutes. Add the bok choi leaves and spring onions, and stir-fry for a further 2 minutes. Stir in the noodles and soy sauce, and season to taste with salt and pepper. Cook until the noodles are heated through, then add the coriander. Serve immediately.

SERVES 4

225 g/8 oz medium egg noodles

3 tbsp groundnut oil

1 large garlic clove, thinly sliced

2 tsp finely chopped fresh ginger

450 g/1 lb turkey steaks, cut into thin strips

175 g/6 oz chestnut mushrooms, thinly sliced

600 g/1 lb 5 oz bok choi, stalks cut into 2.5-cm/1-inch squares and leaves sliced into wide ribbons

4 spring onions, green part included, diagonally sliced into 2.5-cm/1-inch pieces

1 tbsp light soy sauce

2 tbsp chopped fresh coriander

salt and pepper

TURKEY WITH HOISIN SAUCE & CASHEW NUTS

To make the marinade, mix the cornflour and rice wine to a paste. Add the pepper, salt, egg white and sesame oil, mixing well. Put the turkey in a shallow dish and add the marinade, turning to coat. Leave to stand for 30 minutes.

Heat a wok over a high heat, then add 3 tablespoons of the groundnut oil. Add the garlic and white spring onion, and stir for a few seconds to flavour the oil. Add the turkey and reduce the heat slightly. Stir-fry for 2 minutes, until no longer pink, then sprinkle with the rice wine. Transfer to a plate with a slotted spoon.

Increase the heat to high and add the remaining groundnut oil. Swirl the oil around the wok, then stir in the hoisin sauce. Return the turkey mixture to the wok and stir-fry for 2–3 minutes, turning to coat, until cooked through.

Add the cashew nuts and green spring onion. Transfer to a warmed serving dish and serve immediately.

SERVES 4

450 g/1 lb turkey steaks, cubed

4 tbsp groundnut oil

3 large garlic cloves, thinly sliced

4 spring onions, white and green parts separated, diagonally sliced into 2-cm/¾-inch pieces

1 tbsp Chinese rice wine or dry sherry

3 tbsp hoisin sauce

4 tbsp cashew nuts

marinade

1 tsp cornflour

1 tbsp Chinese rice wine or dry sherry

¼ tsp white pepper

½ tsp salt

½ egg white, lightly beaten

2 tsp sesame oil

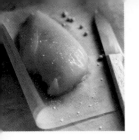

THREE-PEA STIR FRY WITH DUCK

Combine the marinade ingredients in a bowl, stirring to dissolve the sugar. Slice the duck into bite-sized pieces and add to the marinade. Leave to stand at room temperature for 30 minutes, or overnight in the refrigerator.

Heat a wok over a high heat, then add the oil. Stir-fry the white spring onion and the ginger for a few seconds. Add the duck and the marinade, and stir-fry for about 5 minutes. When the liquid has reduced slightly, add the three types of pea and stir-fry for a further 2–3 minutes.

Add the almonds, beansprouts and green spring onion, and stir-fry for a few seconds to heat through. Serve with noodles.

SERVES 4

450 g/1 lb skinless, boneless duck breasts

3 tbsp groundnut oil

6 large spring onions, white and green parts separated, diagonally sliced into 2-cm/ ¾-inch pieces

1 tsp finely chopped fresh ginger

175 g/6 oz sugar snap peas

115 g/4 oz mangetout, diagonally sliced in half

140 g/5 oz shelled peas

3 tbsp whole almonds with skin, halved lengthways

55 g/2 oz fresh breansprouts

freshly cooked noodles, to serve

marinade

1 tbsp light brown sugar

3 tbsp warm water

1–2 fresh red chillies, deseeded and very finely chopped

1 tbsp soy sauce

1 tsp Thai fish sauce

3 tbsp lime juice

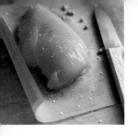

DUCK WITH BLACK BEANS & BROCCOLI

Remove and discard the skin from the duck. Slice the meat into 5-mm/¼-inch strips.

Soak the beans in cold water for 30 minutes, then drain.

Combine the soy sauce, vinegar and sugar in a small bowl, stirring to dissolve the sugar.

Divide the broccoli into florets. Slice the stems very thinly and slice the florets into pieces no more than 2 cm/¾ inch wide.

Heat a wok over a medium heat, then add the oil. Fry the ginger, chilli and garlic for a few seconds to flavour the oil. Add the drained beans, broccoli and red pepper. Increase the heat to high and stir-fry for 2 minutes.

Add the duck and stir-fry for 2 minutes, then add the soy sauce mixture. Continue to stir-fry for a further 2 minutes. Serve immediately.

SERVES 2–3

2 small duck breasts, weighing 450 g/1 lb in total

2 tbsp salted black beans

1½ tbsp soy sauce

1 tbsp rice vinegar

2 tsp sugar

200 g/7 oz broccoli

3 tbsp groundnut oil

2.5-cm/1-inch piece fresh ginger, cut into very thin shreds

1 fresh red chilli, deseeded and thinly sliced diagonally

1 large garlic clove, thinly sliced

½ red pepper, deseeded and thinly sliced

CANTONESE SWEET & SOUR DUCK

Slice each duck breast into 3 pieces and put in a dish. Rub with salt and pepper and the half tablespoon of soy sauce.

Heat a wok over a medium–high heat, then add the oil. Fry the duck for 6 minutes, starting with the skin side down, and turning until brown and crisp on all sides. Using tongs, transfer to a plate and leave to rest in a warm place for 10 minutes. Discard the oil and wipe the wok clean with kitchen paper. Slice the duck into 1-cm/½-inch strips (the meat will still be quite rare at this stage).

To prepare the sauce, mix the cornflour to a smooth paste with 3 tablespoons of the stock. Combine the soy sauce, vinegar and sugar in a small bowl, stirring to dissolve the sugar. Add the tomato purée and orange juice, mixing well.

Heat the oil in the clean wok over a medium heat. Add the ginger slices and stir-fry for a few seconds to flavour the oil. Add the soy sauce mixture and the remaining stock, and bring to the boil. Reduce the heat slightly and add in the cornflour paste. Stir until starting to thicken, then add the duck slices, stirring to coat with the sauce. Simmer over a low heat for 5 minutes, until the duck is cooked but still slightly pink.

Remove the ginger slices and transfer the duck and sauce to a warmed serving dish. Garnish with the cucumber and serve immediately.

SERVES 6

2 boneless duck breasts, skin on, weighing about 550 g/1 lb 4 oz in total

½ tbsp soy sauce

2 tsp groundnut oil

salt and pepper

4-cm/1½-inch piece cucumber, peeled and sliced lengthways into matchsticks, to garnish

sauce

1 tbsp cornflour

125 ml/4 fl oz Basic Chinese Stock (see page 8) or chicken stock

1½ tbsp soy sauce

1½ tbsp rice vinegar

2 tbsp sugar

1 tbsp tomato purée

1 tbsp orange juice

2 tsp groundnut oil

3 thin slices fresh ginger

FISH & SEAFOOD

CHILLIES STUFFED WITH FISH PASTE

Combine all the ingredients for the marinade in a bowl and marinate the fish for 20 minutes. Add the egg and mix by hand to create a smooth paste.

To prepare the chillies, cut in half lengthways and scoop out the seeds and loose flesh. Cut into bite-sized pieces. Spread each piece of chilli with about ½ teaspoon of the fish paste.

Heat a wok over a medium–high heat and add the oil. Cook the chilli pieces on both sides until beginning to turn golden brown. Remove from the oil and set aside.

Heat a clean wok over a medium–high heat and add 1 tablespoon of the oil. Stir-fry the garlic until aromatic. Stir in the black beans and mix well. Add the light soy sauce and sugar and stir, then add the chilli pieces. Add the water, then cover and simmer over a low heat for 5 minutes. Serve immediately.

SERVES 4–6

225 g/8 oz white fish, minced

2 tbsp lightly beaten egg

4–6 mild red and green chillies

vegetable or groundnut oil,
  for shallow-frying

2 garlic cloves, finely chopped

½ tsp fermented black beans,
  rinsed and lightly mashed

1 tbsp light soy sauce

pinch of sugar

1 tbsp water

marinade

1 tsp finely chopped fresh ginger

pinch of salt

pinch of white pepper

½ tsp vegetable or groundnut oil

FRIED FISH WITH PINE KERNELS

Sprinkle the salt over the fish and set aside for 20 minutes. Squeeze out any excess water from the mushrooms and finely slice, discarding any tough stems.

Heat a wok over a medium–high heat and add 2 tablespoons of the oil. Fry the fish for 3 minutes. Drain and set aside.

Heat a clean wok over a medium–high heat and add the remaining oil. Toss in the ginger. Stir until fragrant, then add the spring onions, peppers, bamboo shoots, mushrooms and Shaoxing and cook for 1–2 minutes.

Finally add the fish and stir to warm through. Sprinkle with the pine kernels and serve.

SERVES 4–6

½ tsp salt

450 g/1 lb thick white fish fillets, cut into 2.5-cm/1-inch cubes

2 dried Chinese mushrooms, soaked in warm water for 20 minutes

3 tbsp vegetable or groundnut oil

2.5-cm/1-inch piece of fresh ginger, finely shredded

1 tbsp chopped spring onions

1 red pepper, deseeded and cut into 2.5-cm/1-inch squares

1 green pepper, deseeded and cut into 2.5-cm/1-inch squares

25 g/1 oz fresh or canned bamboo shoots, rinsed and cut into small cubes (if using fresh shoots, boil in water first for 30 minutes)

2 tsp Shaoxing rice wine

2 tbsp pine kernels, toasted

MONKFISH
STIR FRY

Heat a wok over a medium–high heat and add the oil. Add the fish, onion, garlic, ginger, asparagus and mushrooms. Stir-fry for 2–3 minutes.

Stir in the soy sauce and lemon juice and cook for a further minute. Remove from the heat and transfer to serving dishes. Serve immediately.

SERVES 4

2 tsp sesame oil

450 g/1 lb monkfish steaks,
    cut into 2.5-cm/1-inch chunks

1 onion, thinly sliced

3 garlic cloves, finely chopped

1 tsp grated fresh ginger

225 g/8 oz fine tip asparagus

175 g/6 oz mushrooms, thinly
    sliced

2 tbsp soy sauce

1 tbsp lemon juice

STEAMED SALMON WITH BOK CHOI & ASPARAGUS

Place the salmon steaks in a single layer on a heatproof plate that will fit into a wok. Combine the ginger, wine, soy sauce and salt. Sprinkle this over the fish, rubbing it into the flesh, and leave to stand for 20 minutes, turning once.

Snap the woody ends from the asparagus and discard. Cut off the tips and reserve. Chop the stems into 2 or 3 pieces.

Place a trivet in a wok with a lid, and add enough water to come halfway up the trivet. Bring to the boil, then place the plate of fish on the trivet and cover with a loose tent of foil. Adjust the heat so the water is only just boiling. Put the lid on the wok and steam for 10–15 minutes until the fish is opaque and just starting to flake. Meanwhile, heat a second wok over high heat, then add 2 tablespoons of the groundnut oil. Add the asparagus stalks and bok choi, and stir-fry for 4–5 minutes until just tender but still crisp. Splash with a good squeeze of lime juice and season with salt and pepper. Arrange in small mounds on warm serving plates.

Carefully lift the salmon steaks from the wok and place on top of the vegetables. Heat the sesame oil and remaining groundnut oil until very hot. Add the asparagus tips and stir-fry for 20 seconds until barely cooked. Season with coarsely ground black pepper. Arrange the tips on top of the fish and pour the hot oil over the top. Serve at once with rice.

SERVES 4

- 4 salmon steaks, about 2.5 cm/1 inch thick
- 2 tsp finely chopped fresh ginger
- 2 tbsp Chinese rice wine or dry sherry
- 1 tbsp light soy sauce
- ½ tsp salt
- 8 asparagus spears
- 4 tbsp groundnut oil
- 3 heads bok choi, quartered lengthways
- good squeeze of lime juice
- 2 tsp sesame oil
- coarsely ground black pepper
- freshly cooked plain rice, to serve

SALMON & SCALLOPS WITH CORIANDER & LIME

Heat a wok over a medium–high heat and add the oil. Add the salmon and scallops and stir-fry for 3 minutes. Remove from the wok, set aside and keep warm.

Add the carrots, celery, peppers, mushrooms and garlic to the wok and stir-fry for 3 minutes. Add the coriander and shallots and stir.

Add the lime juice and zest, dried red pepper flakes, sherry and soy sauce and stir. Return the salmon and scallops to the wok and stir-fry carefully for another minute. Serve immediately.

SERVES 4

6 tbsp groundnut oil

280 g/10 oz salmon steak, skinned and cut into 2.5-cm/1-inch chunks

225 g/8 oz scallops

3 carrots, thinly sliced

2 celery stalks, cut into 2.5-cm/1-inch pieces

2 yellow peppers, deseeded and thinly sliced

175 g/6 oz oyster mushrooms, thinly sliced

1 garlic clove, crushed

6 tbsp chopped fresh coriander

3 shallots, thinly sliced

juice of 2 limes

1 tsp lime zest

1 tsp dried red pepper flakes

3 tbsp dry sherry

3 tbsp soy sauce

SAUTÉED MACKEREL FILLETS WITH GINGER & SPRING ONIONS

Slice the mackerel fillets in half crossways. Diagonally slash the skin of each piece once or twice. Combine the teaspoon of chopped ginger with the salt. Rub the mixture over both sides of the fish, rubbing it into the slashes and any crevices in the flesh. Leave to stand for 15 minutes.

Combine the sauce ingredients in a small bowl and set aside. Heat a wok over a medium–high heat and add the oil. Dredge the mackerel fillets in the flour and add to the wok. Fry for 4 minutes, turning once. Pour the sauce over the fish, sprinkle with the shredded ginger and spring onions, and fry for a further 2 minutes.

Transfer to a serving dish and sprinkle with a few shreds of Chinese leaves. Serve at once.

SERVES 2–3

- 4 mackerel fillets with skin, weighing about 450 g in total
- 1 tsp finely chopped fresh ginger, plus 2-cm piece finely shredded lengthways
- ½ tsp salt
- 4 tbsp groundnut oil
- 2½ tbsp plain flour
- 3 spring onions, green parts included, sliced
- finely shredded Chinese leaves, to garnish

sauce

- 2 tbsp light soy sauce
- ½ tsp sugar
- 2 tsp Chinese rice wine or dry sherry

SWEET & SOUR FRIED SWORDFISH

Remove and discard the skin from the fish, and slice into bite-sized chunks. Spread out on a plate and sprinkle with the salt. Sieve the flour and cornflour together to get rid of any lumps, then spread out on a plate.

Next make the sauce. Mix the cornflour, sugar and rice vinegar to a smooth paste. Stir in the soy sauce, tomato purée, cooking wine, orange juice and stock. Heat a wok over a medium–high heat and add the oil. Fry the garlic, ginger and spring onion for 1½ minutes. Add the red and green peppers, and stir-fry for 30 seconds. Pour in the cornflour mixture, increase the heat slightly and stir until thickened. Set aside.

Dip the fish in the beaten egg white, then dredge with the flour-cornflour mixture. Heat a wok, preferably non-stick, over a medium–high heat and add the oil and chicken stock. Add the fish and fry for 5–6 minutes, turning to cook each side. Pour in the sauce and simmer for 1–2 minutes, carefully turning the fish so it is coated with the sauce. Serve.

SERVES 2

450 g/1 lb swordfish steaks

1 tsp salt

4 tsp plain flour

4 tsp cornflour

1 egg white, lightly beaten

1½ tbsp groundnut oil

3 tbsp chicken stock

sweet & sour sauce

2 tsp cornflour

1½ tbsp sugar

1½ tbsp rice vinegar

4 tsp soy sauce

4 tsp tomato purée

4 tsp Chinese rice wine or dry sherry

3 tbsp orange juice

3 tbsp chicken stock

2 tsp vegetable oil

1 large garlic clove, crushed

1 tsp finely chopped fresh ginger

2 tbsp chopped spring onion

¼ small red pepper, deseeded and sliced into thin strips

¼ small green pepper, deseeded and sliced into thin strips

SEAFOOD CHOW MEIN

Open up the squid and score the inside in a criss-cross pattern, then cut into pieces about 2.5 cm/1 inch square. Soak the squid in a bowl of boiling water until all the pieces curl up. Rinse in cold water and drain.

Cut each scallop into 3–4 slices. Cut the prawns in half lengthways if large. Mix the scallops and prawns with the egg white and cornflour paste.

Cook the noodles in a saucepan of boiling water for 4 minutes, or according to the instructions on the packet, until soft. Drain well, then toss with about 1 tablespoon of the oil.

Heat a wok over a medium–high heat and add 3 tablespoons of the oil. Add the noodles and 1 tablespoon of the soy sauce and stir-fry for 2–3 minutes. Remove to a large serving dish.

Heat the remaining oil in the wok and add the mangetout and seafood. Stir-fry for about 2 minutes, then add the salt, sugar, rice wine, the remaining soy sauce and about half the spring onions. Blend well and add a little water if necessary. Pour the seafood mixture on top of the noodles and sprinkle with sesame oil. Garnish with the remaining spring onions and serve immediately.

SERVES 4

85 g/3 oz squid, cleaned

3–4 fresh scallops

85 g/3 oz raw prawns, peeled

½ egg white, lightly beaten

2 tsp cornflour, mixed to a paste with 2½ tsp water

275 g/9¾ oz fine egg noodles

5–6 tbsp vegetable oil

2 tbsp light soy sauce

55 g/2 oz mangetout, sliced diagonally

½ tsp salt

½ tsp sugar

1 tsp Chinese rice wine

2 spring onions, finely shredded

a few drops of sesame oil

CLAMS IN BLACK BEAN SAUCE

Discard any clams with broken shells and any that refuse to close when tapped. Wash the remaining clams thoroughly and leave to soak in clean water until ready to cook.

Heat a wok over a medium–high heat and add the oil. Stir-fry the ginger and garlic until fragrant. Add the black beans and cook for 1 minute.

Over a high heat, add the clams and rice wine and stir-fry for 2 minutes to mix everything together. Cover and cook for a further 3 minutes. Add the spring onion and salt, if necessary, and serve immediately.

SERVES 4

900 g/2 lb small clams

1 tbsp vegetable or groundnut oil

1 tsp finely chopped fresh ginger

1 tsp finely chopped garlic

1 tbsp fermented black beans, rinsed and roughly chopped

2 tsp Chinese rice wine

1 tbsp finely chopped spring onion

1 tsp salt (optional)

STIR-FRIED FRESH CRAB WITH GINGER

Heat a wok over a high heat and add 2 tablespoons of the oil. Cook the crab for 3–4 minutes. Remove and set aside. Wipe the wok clean.

In the clean wok, heat the remaining oil, then add the ginger and stir until fragrant. Add the spring onions, then stir in the crab pieces. Add the soy sauce, sugar and pepper. Cover and simmer for 1 minute, then serve immediately.

SERVES 4

3 tbsp vegetable or groundnut oil

2 large fresh crabs, cleaned, broken into pieces, and legs cracked with a cleaver

55 g/2 oz fresh ginger, julienned

100 g/3½ oz spring onions, chopped into 5-cm/2-inch lengths

2 tbsp light soy sauce

1 tsp sugar

pinch of white pepper

SCALLOP, MANGETOUT & MUSHROOM STIR FRY

Heat a wok over a high heat and add the oils. Stir-fry the scallops for
1 minute. Add the mushrooms and mangetout, and stir-fry for a further minute.

   Add the ginger, garlic and soy sauce, and a splash of water to moisten. Stir-fry for another 1–2 minutes until the vegetables are just tender.

   Add the lime juice and coriander leaves, and season to taste. Divide between plates and serve at once.

SERVES 4

3 tbsp groundnut oil

2 tbsp sesame oil

16 large scallops, halved

225 g/8 oz small shiitake mushrooms, tough stalks removed

175 g/6 oz mangetout, trimmed and halved diagonally

2 tsp finely chopped fresh ginger

2 garlic cloves, finely chopped

2 tsp light soy sauce

juice of 1 lime

3 tbsp torn coriander leaves

salt and pepper

PRAWNS FU YUNG

Heat a wok over a high heat and add the oil. Add the prawns and stir-fry for about 4 minutes, or until just pink.

Season the eggs with the salt and pepper and pour over the prawns. Stir-fry for 1 minute, then add the chives.

Cook for a further 4 minutes, stirring all the time, until the eggs are cooked through but still soft in texture. Serve immediately.

SERVES 4–6

1 tbsp vegetable or groundnut oil

115 g/4 oz large prawns, peeled and deveined

4 eggs, lightly beaten

1 tsp salt

pinch of white pepper

2 tbsp finely chopped Chinese chives

SWEET CHILLI SQUID

Place the sesame seeds on a baking sheet, toast under a hot grill and set aside.

Heat a wok over a medium heat and add 1 tablespoon of the oil. Add the squid and cook for 2 minutes, then remove and set aside.

Add another 1 tablespoon of the oil to the frying pan and fry the peppers and shallots over a medium heat for 1 minute. Add the mushrooms and fry for a further 2 minutes.

Return the squid to the frying pan and add the sherry, soy sauce, sugar, chilli flakes and garlic, stirring thoroughly. Cook for a further 2 minutes.

Sprinkle with the toasted sesame seeds, drizzle over the remaining sesame oil and mix. Serve on a bed of rice.

SERVES 4

1 tbsp sesame seeds, toasted

2⅓ tbsp sesame oil

280 g/10 oz squid, cut into strips

2 red peppers, deseeded and thinly sliced

3 shallots, thinly sliced

85 g/3 oz mushrooms, thinly sliced

1 tbsp dry sherry

4 tbsp soy sauce

1 tsp sugar

1 tsp hot chilli flakes, or to taste

1 clove of garlic, crushed

freshly cooked plain rice, to serve

TIGER PRAWNS IN TAMARIND SAUCE

Remove the shells from the prawns leaving the last segment and the tail in place. Combine the ginger, shallots and chilli in a small bowl. Combine the sauce ingredients in another bowl.

Heat a wok over a high heat, then add the oil. When the oil is almost smoking, add the prawns and stir-fry for 3–4 minutes until just pink. Remove from the wok and drain in a colander.

Pour off all but 2 tablespoons of oil from the wok. Heat the remaining oil over a high heat and stir-fry the ginger mixture for 1 minute. Add the tamarind sauce and stir for a few seconds until hot. Add the prawns and stir-fry for 1 minute until the sauce is slightly reduced.

Transfer the prawns to a warm serving dish and sprinkle with the coriander. Serve with rice.

SERVES 2

350 g raw headless tiger prawns, unshelled

1½ tbsp finely chopped fresh ginger

2 shallots, finely chopped

½ green chilli, deseeded and finely chopped

groundnut oil, for frying

3 tbsp chopped fresh coriander, to garnish

freshly cooked plain rice, to serve

tamarind sauce

1 tbsp tamarind paste

1 tbsp sugar

2 tsp oyster sauce

2 tbsp water

1 tsp fish sauce

VEGETARIAN

HOT & SOUR COURGETTES

Put the courgette slices in a large colander and toss with the salt. Cover with a plate and put a weight on top. Leave to drain for 20 minutes. Rinse off the salt and spread out the slices on kitchen paper to dry.

Heat a wok over a high heat and add the groundnut oil. Add the Szechuan pepper, chilli, garlic and ginger. Fry for about 20 seconds until the garlic is just beginning to colour.

Add the courgette slices and toss in the oil. Add the rice vinegar, soy sauce and sugar, and stir-fry for 2 minutes. Add the spring onion and fry for 30 seconds. Sprinkle with the sesame oil and seeds, and serve immediately.

SERVES 4

2 large courgettes, thinly sliced

1 tsp salt

2 tbsp groundnut oil

1 tsp Szechuan pepper, crushed

½ –1 red chilli, deseeded and sliced into thin strips

1 large garlic clove, thinly sliced

½ tsp finely chopped fresh ginger

1 tbsp rice vinegar

1 tbsp light soy sauce

2 tsp sugar

1 spring onion, green part included, thinly sliced

a few drops of sesame oil, to garnish

1 tsp sesame seeds, to garnish

AUBERGINE STIR FRY WITH HOT & SOUR SAUCE

VEGETARIAN

164

First prepare the sauce. Combine the soy sauce, rice vinegar and sugar in a small bowl, stirring to dissolve the sugar. Mix in the cornflour paste and stir until smooth.

Heat the stock and set aside.

Slice the aubergines in half lengthways. With the flat side facing down, slice each half lengthways into 1-cm/½-inch strips. Slice the wider strips lengthways in half again, then cut all the strips crossways into 4-cm/1½-inch pieces.

Heat a wok over a high heat and add 5 tablespoons of the oil. Add the aubergine and red pepper strips and stir-fry for 2–3 minutes until just beginning to colour. Remove from the wok and drain on kitchen paper.

Heat the remaining tablespoon of oil over a high heat. Stir-fry the water chestnuts, spring onions, ginger, garlic and chilli for 1 minute.

Return the aubergine and red pepper to the wok. Reduce the heat to medium, and add soy sauce and the stock. Stir-fry for 2–3 minutes until slightly thickened. Sprinkle with sesame seeds and sliced spring onion tops. Serve with rice.

SERVES 4

150 ml/5 fl oz vegetable stock

2 aubergines, peeled

6 tbsp groundnut oil

2 red peppers, deseeded and cut into matchstick strips

100 g/3½ oz canned drained water chestnuts, sliced

6 spring onions, sliced

2 tsp finely chopped fresh ginger

1 large garlic clove, thinly sliced

1 green chilli, deseeded and finely chopped

salt and pepper

1 tsp sesame seeds and thinly sliced spring onion tops, to garnish

freshly cooked plain rice, to serve

sauce

1½ tbsp soy sauce

1½ tbsp rice vinegar

2 tsp sugar

2 tsp cornflour, blended to a smooth paste with a little water

BROCCOLI WITH PEANUTS

Put 2 tablespoons of the oil, the lemon grass, chillies, ginger, lime leaves and curry paste into a food processor or blender and process to a paste.

Heat a wok over a medium heat and add the remaining oil. Add the spice paste, onion and red pepper and stir-fry for 2–3 minutes, until the vegetables start to soften.

Add the broccoli and French beans, cover and cook over a low heat, stirring occasionally, for 4–5 minutes, until tender.

Meanwhile, toast or dry-fry the peanuts until lightly browned. Add them to the broccoli mixture and toss together. Serve immediately.

SERVES 4

3 tbsp vegetable or groundnut oil

1 lemon grass stem, roughly chopped

2 fresh red chillies, deseeded and chopped

2.5-cm/1-inch piece fresh ginger, grated

3 kaffir lime leaves, roughly torn

3 tbsp Thai green curry paste

1 onion, chopped

1 red pepper, deseeded and chopped

350 g/12 oz broccoli, cut into florets

115 g/4 oz French beans

55 g/2 oz unsalted peanuts

MUSHROOMS & FRENCH BEANS WITH LEMON & CORIANDER

Rinse the mushrooms and dry with kitchen paper. If using clumping mushrooms, such as enoki and buna shimeji, slice off the root and separate the clump. Slice cremini mushrooms in half.

Heat a wok over a medium–high heat and add the oil. Add the coriander seeds and bay leaf, and fry for a few seconds to flavour the oil. Add the mushrooms and beans, and stir-fry for 5 minutes.

Stir in the garlic, lemon juice and soy sauce. Season with salt and pepper, and stir-fry for 2 minutes. Sprinkle with the coriander, sesame oil and seeds, and fry for a few seconds. Serve hot, warm or at room temperature.

SERVES 2

450 g/1 lb mixed small mushrooms such as cremini, enoki and buna shimeji

6 tbsp rapeseed oil

1 tsp coriander seeds, crushed

1 fresh bay leaf

175 g/6 oz French beans

1 large garlic clove, thinly sliced

3 tbsp lemon juice

2 tsp soy sauce

2 tbsp chopped coriander

2 tsp sesame oil

2 tsp sesame seeds

salt and pepper

SPICY TOFU
WITH RICE

Combine all the marinade ingredients in a bowl. Add the tofu and toss well to cover in the marinade. Set aside to marinate for 20 minutes.

Heat a wok over a medium–high heat and add 2 tablespoons of the oil. Stir-fry the tofu with its marinade until brown and crispy. Remove from the wok and set aside.

Heat the remaining 2 tablespoons of oil in the wok and stir-fry the ginger, garlic and spring onions for 30 seconds. Add the broccoli, carrot, yellow pepper and mushrooms and cook for 5–6 minutes. Return the tofu to the wok and stir-fry to reheat. Serve immediately with rice.

SERVES 6

250 g/9 oz firm tofu, rinsed, drained and cut into 1-cm/½-inch cubes

4 tbsp groundnut oil

1 tbsp grated fresh ginger

3 garlic cloves, crushed

4 spring onions, thinly sliced

1 head of broccoli, cut into florets

1 carrot, cut into batons

1 yellow pepper, deseeded and thinly sliced

250 g/9 oz shiitake mushrooms, thinly sliced

freshly cooked plain rice, to serve

marinade

5 tbsp vegetable stock

2 tsp cornflour

2 tbsp light soy sauce

1 tbsp caster sugar

pinch of chilli flakes

OYSTER MUSHROOMS & VEGETABLES WITH PEANUT CHILLI SAUCE

Heat a wok over a high heat, add the oil and heat until almost smoking. Stir-fry the spring onions for 1 minute. Add the carrot and courgette and stir-fry for another minute. Then add the broccoli and cook for a further minute.

Stir in the mushrooms and cook until they are soft and at least half the liquid they produce has evaporated. Add the peanut butter and stir well, then season with the chilli powder to taste. Finally add the water and cook for 1 minute.

Garnish with lime wedges and serve with rice.

SERVES 6

1 tbsp vegetable or groundnut oil

4 spring onions, finely sliced

1 carrot, cut into thin strips

1 courgette, cut into thin strips

½ head of broccoli, cut into florets

450 g/1 lb oyster mushrooms, thinly sliced

2 tbsp crunchy peanut butter

1 tsp chilli powder, or to taste

3 tbsp water

lime wedges, to garnish

freshly cooked plain rice, to serve

ASIAN VEGETABLES WITH YELLOW BEAN SAUCE

Cut the aubergine into 5-cm/2-inch-long thin sticks. Place in a colander, then sprinkle with salt and let stand for 30 minutes. Rinse in cold water and dry thoroughly with kitchen paper.

Heat a wok over a medium–high heat and add the oil. Add the garlic, spring onions and pepper and stir-fry over a high heat for 1 minute. Stir in the aubergine pieces and stir-fry for a further minute, or until softened.

Stir in the baby corn and mangetout and stir-fry for 1 minute. Add the bok choi, mushrooms and beansprouts and stir-fry for 30 seconds.

Mix the rice wine, yellow bean sauce, soy sauce, chilli sauce and sugar together in a bowl, then add to the pan with the stock. Bring to the boil, stirring constantly.

Slowly blend the cornflour with the water to form a smooth paste, then stir quickly into the pan and cook for a further minute. Serve immediately.

VEGETARIAN

174

SERVES 4

1 aubergine

salt

2 tbsp vegetable oil

3 garlic cloves, crushed

4 spring onions, chopped

1 small red pepper, deseeded and thinly sliced

4 baby corn, halved lengthways

115 g/4 oz mangetout

200 g/7 oz green bok choi, coarsely shredded

425 g/14½ oz canned straw mushrooms, drained

115 g/4 oz fresh beansprouts

2 tbsp Chinese rice wine or dry sherry

2 tbsp yellow bean sauce

2 tbsp dark soy sauce

1 tsp chilli sauce

1 tsp sugar

150 ml/5 fl oz vegetable stock

1 tsp cornflour

2 tsp water

SPICY NOODLES WITH MUSHROOM EGG ROLLS

Heat a wok over a medium–high heat and add 1 tablespoon of the oil. Stir-fry the onion and mushrooms until crisp and browned. Add the curry paste and soy sauce and stir-fry for 2–3 minutes. Remove the wok from the heat.

Spoon an eighth of the mixture across one of the egg roll skins and roll up, folding the sides over the filling to enclose it.

Clean the wok and heat over a high heat. Pour in the oil and heat to 180°C/350°F or until a cube of bread browns in 30 seconds. Deep-fry the egg rolls, 4 at a time, until crisp and browned. Drain on kitchen paper and keep warm.

Meanwhile, put the noodles in a bowl, cover with boiling water and set aside to swell.

Heat the remaining oil in the wok and stir-fry the garlic, spring onions and red pepper for 2–3 minutes. Stir in the coriander and cumin, then drain the noodles and add them to the wok. Toss together and serve topped with the egg rolls.

SERVES 4

2 tbsp vegetable or groundnut oil

1 small onion, chopped finely

225 g/8 oz mushrooms, chopped

1 tbsp Thai red curry paste

1 tbsp Thai soy sauce

8 square egg roll skins

vegetable or groundnut oil, for deep-frying

225 g/8 oz quick-cook noodles

1 garlic clove, chopped

6 spring onions, chopped

1 red pepper, deseeded and chopped

1 tbsp ground coriander

1 tbsp ground cumin

MUSHROOM & TOFU LAKSA WITH NOODLES

Purée the spice paste ingredients in a food processor, pulsing several times until smooth.

Heat a wok over a medium–high heat, add the spice paste and stir-fry for 30 seconds. Pour in the stock and coconut milk, and bring to the boil. Add the mushrooms, tofu and tomato purée and season with salt and pepper. Simmer gently for 5 minutes.

Cook the noodles in a saucepan of boiling water for 4 minutes, or according to the instructions on the packet, until soft. Divide between four large soup bowls. Ladle the spicy broth over the noodles. Serve with the garnishes.

SERVES 4

850 ml/1½ pints vegetable stock

400 g/14 oz canned coconut milk

250 g/9 oz shiitake mushrooms, stalks removed, thinly sliced

150 g/5¼ oz firm tofu, cubed

2 tbsp tomato purée

175 g/6 oz fine egg noodles

salt and pepper

8 spring onions, sliced, and 4 tbsp shredded mint leaves, to garnish

spice paste

2 red chillies, deseeded and chopped

4 cm/1½ inch piece fresh ginger, chopped

2 large garlic cloves, chopped

2 lemon grass stems, tough outer layers discarded, inner stalks chopped

1 tsp coriander seeds, crushed

6 macadamia nuts, chopped

small handful of coriander leaves

3 tbsp vegetable oil

BROCCOLI & MANGETOUT STIR FRY

Heat a wok over a medium–high heat and add the oils. Add the garlic and stir-fry vigorously. Add all the vegetables and salt and stir-fry over a high heat, tossing rapidly, for about 3 minutes.

Pour in the soy sauce and rice wine and cook for a further 2 minutes. Sprinkle with the sesame seeds and serve hot.

SERVES 4

2 tbsp vegetable or groundnut oil

dash of sesame oil

1 garlic clove, finely chopped

225 g/8 oz small head of broccoli, broken into florets

115 g/4 oz mangetout

225 g/8 oz Chinese leaves, chopped into 1-cm/½-inch slices

5–6 spring onions, finely chopped

½ tsp salt

2 tbsp light soy sauce

1 tbsp Chinese rice wine

1 tsp sesame seeds, lightly toasted, to garnish

RED CURRY WITH MIXED LEAVES

Heat a wok over a medium–high heat and add the oil. Add the onions and asparagus and stir-fry for 1–2 minutes.

Add the coconut milk, curry paste and lime leaves and bring gently to the boil, stirring occasionally. Add the spinach, bok choi and Chinese leaves and cook, stirring, for 2–3 minutes, until wilted. Add the coriander and stir well. Serve immediately with rice.

SERVES 4

2 tbsp groundnut or vegetable oil

2 onions, thinly sliced

1 bunch of fine asparagus spears

400 ml/14 fl oz coconut milk

2 tbsp Thai red curry paste

3 fresh kaffir lime leaves

225 g/8 oz baby spinach leaves

2 heads bok choi, chopped

1 small head Chinese leaves, shredded

handful of fresh coriander, chopped

freshly cooked plain rice, to serve

CARROT & PUMPKIN CURRY

Pour the stock into a large saucepan and bring to the boil. Add the galangal, half the garlic, the lemon grass and chillies and simmer for 5 minutes. Add the carrots and pumpkin and simmer for 5–6 minutes, until tender.

Heat a wok over a medium–high heat and add the oil. Stir-fry the shallots and the remaining garlic for 2–3 minutes. Add the curry paste and stir-fry for 1–2 minutes.

Stir the shallot mixture into the saucepan and add the coconut milk and Thai basil. Simmer for 2–3 minutes. Serve hot, sprinkled with the toasted pumpkin seeds.

SERVES 4

150 ml/5 fl oz vegetable stock

2.5-cm/1-inch piece fresh galangal, sliced

2 garlic cloves, chopped

1 lemon grass stem (white part only), finely chopped

2 fresh red chillies, deseeded and chopped

4 carrots, peeled and cut into chunks

225 g/8 oz pumpkin, peeled, deseeded and cut into cubes

2 tbsp vegetable or groundnut oil

2 shallots, finely chopped

3 tbsp Thai yellow curry paste

400 ml/14 fl oz coconut milk

4–6 fresh Thai basil sprigs

25 g/1 oz toasted pumpkin seeds, to garnish

CABBAGE & COCONUT CURRY

Purée the spice paste ingredients in a food processor or blender, adding a splash of water to moisten.

Heat a wok over a medium–high heat and add the oil. Fry the mustard seeds until they start to crackle. Reduce the heat to medium, then add the onion and stir-fry until golden. Stir in the spice paste and fry for 30 seconds.

Add the shredded white and green cabbage and pour in the water, stirring well so the cabbage is covered with the paste. Season with the crushed peppercorns and a little salt. Cover and cook over low heat for 7–10 minutes, stirring now and again to prevent sticking.

When the cabbage is tender, add the coconut flakes, coriander and lime juice. Stir for a minute to heat through and serve.

SERVES 4–6

3 tbsp vegetable oil

1 tsp mustard seeds

1 small onion sliced

¼ white cabbage, core removed, leaves shredded

½ small green cabbage, core removed, leaves shredded

100–125 ml/3–4 fl oz water

½ tsp black peppercorns, crushed

4 tbsp toasted coconut flakes

3 tbsp chopped coriander leaves

juice of ½ lime

salt

spice paste

50 g sachet creamed coconut, melted

1 green chilli, deseeded and roughly chopped

1 tbsp finely chopped fresh ginger

2 garlic cloves, sliced

1 small onion, finely chopped

½ tsp salt

1 tsp cumin seeds

½ tsp ground turmeric

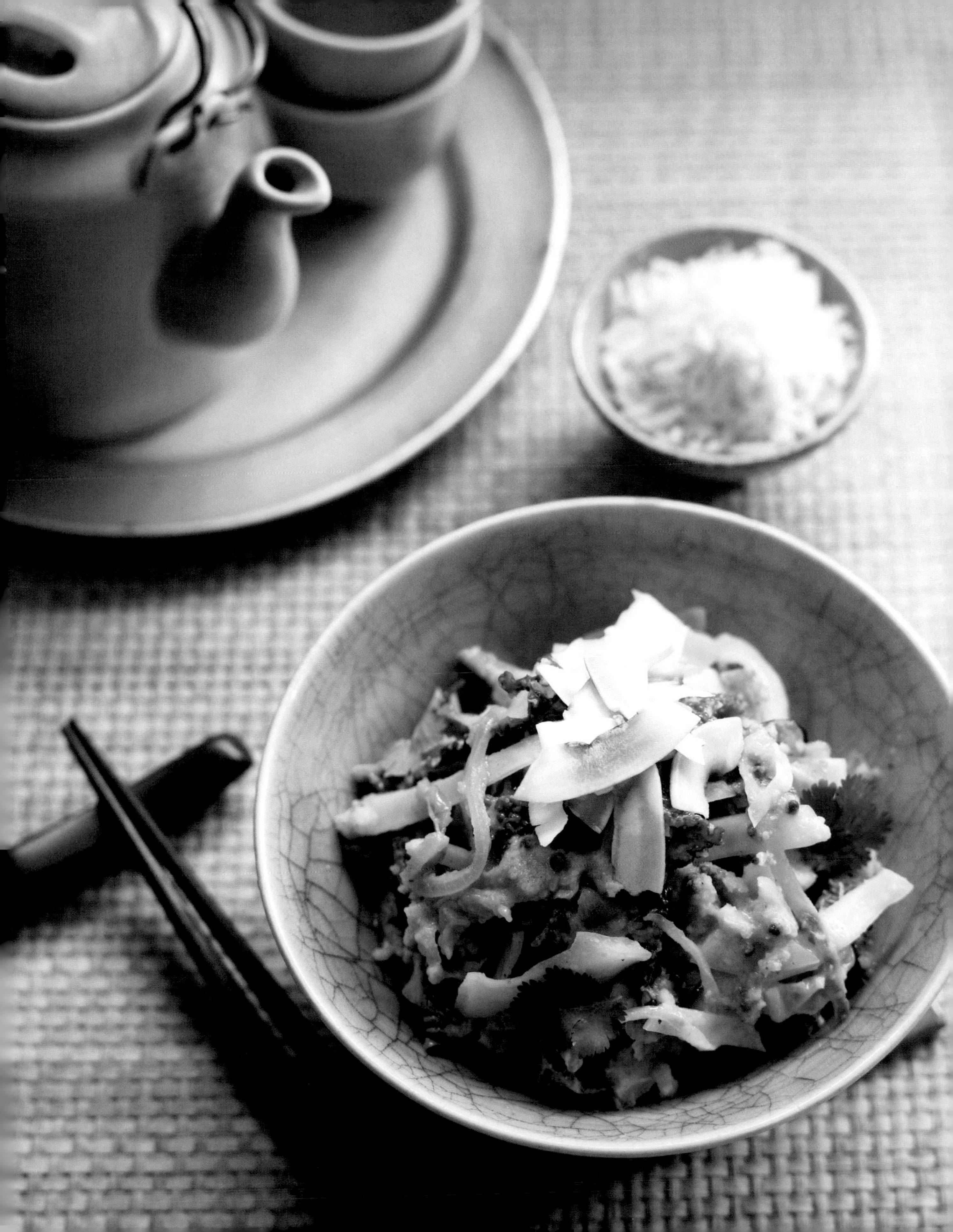

EGG FU YUNG

Beat the eggs with the salt and pepper. Heat the butter in a frying pan and pour in the eggs. Cook as an omelette, until set, then remove from the pan and cut into slivers.

   Heat a wok over a medium–high heat and add the oil. Stir-fry the garlic until fragrant. Add the onion and stir-fry for 1 minute, then add the green pepper and stir-fry for a further 1 minute. Stir in the rice and, when the grains are separated, stir in the light soy sauce and cook for 1 minute.

   Add the spring onions and egg strips and stir well, then add the beansprouts and sesame oil. Stir-fry for 1 minute and serve.

SERVES 4–6

2 eggs

½ tsp salt

pinch of white pepper

1 tsp melted butter

2 tbsp vegetable or groundnut oil

1 tsp finely chopped garlic

1 small onion, finely sliced

1 green pepper, deseeded and finely sliced

450 g/1 lb cooked rice, chilled

1 tbsp light soy sauce

1 tbsp finely chopped spring onions

150 g/5 oz fresh beansprouts, trimmed

2 drops of sesame oil

INDEX